Expectation
The Very Brief Therapy Book

Rubin Battino

MS, Mental Health Counseling
Adjunct Professor, Department of Human Services (Counseling)
Wright State University

Crown House Publishing Limited
www.crownhouse.co.uk

First published by

Crown House Publishing Ltd
Crown Buildings, Bancyfelin, Carmarthen, Wales, SA33 5ND, UK
www.crownhouse.co.uk

and

Crown House Publishing Company LLC
4 Berkeley Street, 1st Floor, Norwalk, CT 06850, USA
www.CHPUS.com

British Library of Cataloguing-in-Publication Data
A catalogue entry for this book is available from the British Library.

10-digit ISBN 1845900286
13-digit ISBN 978-184590028-1

LCCN 2006923155

Printed and bound in the UK by
Cromwell Press
Trowbridge
Wiltshire

Acknowledgments

The author and publisher gratefully acknowledge the permission granted to reproduce copyright material in this book (exact citations given throughout the text) from the following sources:

American Psychological Association

Excerpts from *The heart & soul of change: What works in therapy* by M. A. Hubble, B. L. Duncan and S. D. Miller (eds) are copyright © 1999 by the American Psychological Association. Reprinted with permission.

Brunner/Mazel (Taylor & Francis Group)

All excerpts in Chapter 12 are copyright © 1998 from *Nature-guided therapy: Brief integrative strategies for health and well-being* by G. W. Burns. Reproduced by permission of Routledge/Taylor & Francis Group, LLC.

All excerpts in Chapter 11 are copyright © 1986 from *Enchantment and intervention in family therapy: Training in Ericksonian approaches* by S. R. Lankton and C. H. Lankton. Reproduced by permission of Routledge/Taylor & Francis Group, LLC.

Crown House Publishing Limited

Battino, R., 2002, *Metaphoria: Metaphor and guided metaphor for psychotherapy and healing*. Carmarthen, UK: Crown House Publishing.

Battino, R., and South, T. L., 2005, *Ericksonian approaches: A comprehensive manual*. (2nd edn.). Carmarthen, UK: Crown House Publishing.

Bodenhamer, B. G., and Hall, L. M., 1999, *The user's manual for the brain: The complete manual for neuro-linguistic programming practitioner certification*. Carmarthen, UK: Crown House Publishing.

Derks, L., 2005, *Social panoramas: Changing the unconscious landscape with NLP and psychotherapy*. Carmarthen, UK: Crown House Publishing.

Hall, L. M., and Bodenhamer, B. G., 2003, *The user's manual for the brain Volume II: Mastering systemic NLP*. Carmarthen, UK: Crown House Publishing.

Kane, S., and Olness, K. (eds), 2004, *The art of therapeutic communication: The collected works of Kay F. Thompson*. Carmarthen, UK: Crown House Publishing.

Ernest Rossi
Rossi, E. L., 1996, *The symptom path to enlightenment: The new dynamics of self-organization in hypnotherapy: An advanced manual for beginners*. Pacific Palisades, CA: Palisades Gateway Publishing.

John Wiley & Sons, Inc.
Excerpts from *The heroic client: A revolutionary way to improve effectiveness through client-directed, outcome-informed therapy* are copyright © 2004 B. L. Duncan, S. D. Miller and J. A. Sparks. Reprinted with permission of John Wiley & Sons, Inc.

Excerpts from *Single-session therapy: Maximizing the effect of the first (and often only) therapeutic encounter* are copyright ©1990 M. Talmon. Reprinted with permission of John Wiley & Sons, Inc.

Lawrence Erlbaum Associates, Inc.
Wampold, B. E., 2001, *The great psychotherapy debate: Models, methods and findings*. Mahwah, NJ: Lawrence Erlbaum Associates, Publishers.

W. W. Norton & Company
Excerpts from *The miracle method: A radically new approach to problem drinking* by Scott D. Miller and Insoo Kim Berg. Copyright © 1995 by Scott D. Miller and Insoo Kim Berg. Used by permission of W. W. Norton & Company, Inc.

Excerpts from *My voice will go with you: The teaching tales of Milton H. Erickson* by Milton H. Erickson and Sidney Rosen, M.D. Copyright © 1982 by Sidney Rosen, M.D. Used by permission of W. W. Norton & Company, Inc.

Excerpts from *A guide to inclusive therapy: 26 methods of respectful, resistance-dissolving therapy* by Bill O'Hanlon. Copyright © 2003 by Bill O'Hanlon. Used by permission of W. W. Norton & Company, Inc.

Every effort has been made to trace copyright holders and to obtain their permission for the use of copyright material. The author and publisher apologize for any errors or omission and would be grateful if notified ot any corrections that should be incorporated in future reprints or editions of this book.

Contents

Foreword

Long Days Journey into Light

Reading Rubin Battino's book *Expectation: The Very Brief Therapy Book* brought to mind a personal experience regarding the potential impact of brief therapeutic encounters. Some twenty years ago, I was a graduate student, plodding through my remaining classes, conducting dissertation research, while struggling to make ends meet through a combination of student loans and a graduate assistantship. I was also several years into my own psychoanalysis. Three and sometimes four times a week, I drove the ten-mile stretch from the University to my analyst's office. Once there, I waited patiently in the anteroom listening to classic music until my analyst would appear and invite me into the salon.

The nature of the treatment had not changed for several years. I would lie on a couch, my head resting on a clean white linen napkin neatly laid out following the last patient. Then I would talk: about my family, my childhood, school, my marriage, my dreams and, of course, my fantasies. Meanwhile, my analyst—a graying, grandfatherly kind of fellow trained in the Winnicot School—sat behind me, chin in hand with one leg crossed at the knee (I know because I almost always found a reason to sit up once a session to look at him for a response or add emphasis to what I was saying).

At some point during this process, I'd started keeping a dream journal. Desperately hoping to be a "good" and cooperative patient, I left nothing out. As a result, the collection of spiral bound notebooks containing lengthy recollections or mere fragments grew tremendously over time. And while I was (and still am) not an artistic person, I even started sketching my dreams, bringing them to my sessions and, in my spare time, arranging and re-arranging the drawings in an attempt to plumb the darker recesses of my unconscious.

Originally, I'd entered analysis as a way of bolstering my experience and knowledge about treatment. I was not depressed or anxious and both my upbringing and life experience were more akin to *Leave it to Beaver* than say, *Nightmare on Elm Street*. But I was a young graduate student—younger and less experienced than most of the others in my cohort. Nearly all of the students in my class, for example, either were or had been in therapy. A significant number were already working in the field. Alas, I felt the need to "catch up," and do so with alacrity. Psychoanalysis seemed to fit the bill. What's more, the rigorous, driven, "leave no stone unturned" quality of the approach appealed to me personally.

Several years into the experience, however, I became depressed—so much so that the number of times per week I went to therapy was stepped up and I started taking anti-depressant medication. The almost limitless enthusiasm I'd had for life and learning drained away. It was all I could do to make it to classes and work. I became increasingly isolated, rarely interacting more than was necessary with schoolmates or work associates. When my marriage finally started to unravel, I found myself struggling daily with thoughts I'd never had before: I wanted to be dead.

It was around this time that I had a life-changing experience. The incident was neither planned nor expected, but I believe it did save my life. As part of my work as a graduate assistant, I helped with the planning and organization of continuing education events for the local chapter of a national professional organization. The work wasn't particularly glamorous—mostly, I pasted mailing labels on brochures and collated them for bulk-rate shipping—but I was, as a result, able to attend trainings featuring cutting-edge practitioners and researchers without having to pay the price of admission.

As fate would have it, I attended a two-day workshop on the subject of brief therapy. I listened attentively to the presenter whose style was not only entertaining and engaging but his message quite provocative: *effective therapy could be and was, in most instances, relatively short in duration.* I learned about Milton H. Erickson, Jay Haley, and the Mental Research Institute (MRI). Videotape of real sessions and role plays with audience members were used to demonstrate various principles and practices. And while the details of those two days are now a blur, I remember coming away from the experience with a profound appreciation of the role that language and expectation play in the process of change.

By the end of the two days, I'd decided to contact the presenter for help. Being a compulsive person, my idea was to get enough "brief therapy" to resolve my depression so that I could finish my analysis. Although the setting was quite different—I had to sit in a waiting room full of other people seeking help in a rather sterile-looking professional office building located in what amounted to a strip mall—the hour long session did not strike me as all that remarkable. We sat face-to-face, the therapist listened attentively and asked lots of questions. Near the end of the interview, he took what he called a "break", leaving the room temporarily, he said, "to reflect on the visit and collect his thoughts" before making some suggestions.

I was writing a check for the hour when he returned. "I've given this some thought," he said, "and have an idea."

"Great," I either said or thought. "Let's hear it."

"Are you interested?" he asked.

"Yeah," I said with a pained laugh. "Of course."

"Because," he then continued, "you've got a lot going on right now, and I don't want to burden you."

"I'm interested, really ... anything you can tell me," I said. "... I'm drowning here."

"With everything that's going on, this may sound a little odd, though, even crazy."

Not being sure I understood, I shook my head and then said, "I've got to do something."

"OK, then," he continued, "here it is. When you go to work tomorrow, to your office, I'd like you to go over to the window near your desk and *roll the blinds open* … or, if *you are tempted, pull the shades up* completely."

I must have stared blankly at him for more than a few seconds because he soon asked me if I'd understood him and then, even though I'd said I had, he repeated the very same instructions once or twice more. But what perhaps appeared to him as incoherence on my part was actually shock. "Of course, I heard it," I thought privately to myself. "I'm not an idiot. I'm an advanced, doctoral-level graduate student." What I wanted to do was shout, "That's it? Roll up the Blinds? Pull up the Shades? That cost 90 bucks? Geez."

That night doom accompanied and intensified my usual gloom. Something was different that's for sure. I was *mad* or, given the current company of readers better said, angry. I felt cheated. Graduate school wasn't teaching me anything I could use to help myself. I'd now spent years talking about my mother, my dreams, fantasies and so on—all to no avail. And now, this guy tells me to pull up my shades. "Our profession sucks!" I thought as I prepared for and then went to bed.

The next morning, I drove into the city, fighting traffic while brooding over the previous day's events. In my memory, I picture other drivers catching a glimpse of me complete with a cartoon-like bubble hanging over my head with "&%$#!" written visibly inside. My mood would certainly have been obvious to anyone who watched me exit my car that day and stomp up the walkway to my office. Sitting down, I followed my usual routine. I turned on the low wattage light fixture that sat on my desk, leaned back in my chair and began looking over the series of hand-drawn dream images currently hanging on the wall.

My attempt to wring some life-changing insight out of my dreams kept being interrupted by thoughts about the previous day. Every now and then I'd turn toward the Levelor® blinds covering the window adjacent to my desk. Rolling my eyes, I'd think, "Pull up the shades, ha! What humbug." Eventually, however, I thought, "Ah, what the heck," and reached out, grabbed the rod next to the shades, and began turning. Immediately, light came flooding into the office. I watched transfixed as people walked the pathways around and into the building—sometimes alone, often in pairs, thinking, laughing, being, eating and talking. Birds flitted from tree to tree. Squirrels chased each other or perched high on tree limbs nibbling some newly found treasure. And when I spontaneously cranked open the office window, the sounds of this life happening outside the narrow confines of my office filled the room.

Suffice it to say, the experience was "eye opening". In the weeks following, I spent more and more time looking outward rather than inward. My energy quickly returned and the depression disappeared. Beyond the impact on my personal wellbeing, however, that very brief encounter—a single session—actually changed the direction of my entire career. Of course, following my experience, I wanted to know, "How did he know to do that?" Together with my colleagues, I've spent the last 20 years writing about and conducting research on the qualities of effective therapy and therapists.

Much of what we and others have found, and more, is collected, summarized, and illustrated in this concise, clearly written volume by Rubin Battino. The book reflects his knowledge and experience assembled over many years of clinical practice in a real-world clinical setting. As such, it is a treasure. Moreover, in addition to providing specific ideas and strategies for helping clients, it provides a platform for raising the hopes of clinicians working during a time in the history of the field when more is expected for less. Take the book, find yourself a comfortable chair next to a window, pull up the blinds, and expect to change.

Scott D. Miller, PhD
Chicago, Illinois
www.talkingcure.com

Introduction

A number of years ago, I heard an impressive talk by the psychologist Moshe Talmon on single-session therapy. I even had the privilege of spending some time chatting with him over a meal. His book on the subject (1990) and the talk contain three startling revelations about the process of doing psychotherapy. Talmon did the unusual thing of studying the records of the large health maintenance organization he worked for. His first discovery was that the most common number of sessions for the large number of clients the psychotherapy staff saw was *one*. The second revelation was that there was no apparent connection between the orientation of the therapist, i.e., the type of psychotherapy they used in their practice, *or* with a particular therapist. That is, the modal length of therapy for every one of the therapists was a single session. Moreover, thirty per cent of the patients chose to come for only one session in the period of one year. (I will be writing more later about the research that shows that the therapist's orientation has little to do with outcome.) The third revelation had to do with follow-up phone calls by neutral staff members. The patients were asked if they were satisfied with the therapy they received. Then they were asked to tell the caller what it was that the therapist did that was so helpful. Independently, the therapists were asked to consult their case notes (this is six months to one year later) and to relate what it was that they thought they did in the session that was helpful to the client. Again, in the judgment of the therapist, what had they done that was critical in helping the client? You may or may not be surprised to discover that there was essentially zero correlation between what the client said helped them and what the therapist thought was important! A reasonable conclusion from this is that it is the client's expectations and attitude that are the important elements of successful therapy.

This brings me to the subject of this book. It is simply how I work as a very brief therapist. My hope is that you will learn some useful ways of working fast and effectively. By "very brief" I mean that I rarely see my clients more than one or two times—usually it is just once. (They do know that I will see them as many times as they feel that meeting with me will be helpful.) I do get feedback sporadically, and it has been uniformly positive. It is my *expectation* that each session is the last one, and that generally one session is all that is needed. Of course, working for myself, my sessions are always open-ended and can last a long time. That is, there is no time constraint on a session. Given *my* expectation and belief in a single session, it is natural that the client accepts this, and that the session is full of meaningful work for the client. My intake form is quite simple, I do not do testing or diagnoses, and we get right down to work. As a related illustration, I recall some comments the psychologist Joseph Barber made about working with clients who have migraines. In effect, he tells them that their body already knows how to stop the migraine because it invariably does so after some period of time. Since this is invariably the case, the client must agree with this statement. Barber's question (and suggestion) to the client is, "Since your body already knows how to end the migraine, why wait one, two, or three days to do this when you can actually do it in the next hour, or even the next few minutes?" Change the frame and change the expectation. So, throughout this book, the idea of "expectation" will be prominently featured.

Chapter 1 is not only an introduction to the book and the idea of doing very brief therapy, but it is also a summary of significant research on this subject. In particular, the work of Miller, Duncan, Hubble and associates, and that of Wampold will be highlighted. What has emerged from their research is evidence supporting what I cited above as Talmon's "revelations". In effect, the clients and their attitudes and expectations are the central key to all psychotherapeutic work. I will be writing more about this later, yet I must insert here the bit of wisdom some group leader in my early training gave, "When all else fails, ask the client what will work." Perhaps, this should be done *before* "all else fails"!

In Chapter 2, I discuss the ideas of expectation as applied to psychotherapy, and also the power of As-If. Also covered are the theory of change and reframing. The therapeutic alliance has been written and spoken about as being central to change work, so

Chapter 3 briefly covers rapport-building skills. That is, it is useful if the client believes that you both exist in the world in somehow and somewhat similar ways.

Being restricted to "talk" therapy by not being a physician means that the psychotherapist needs to rely on language to help a client find ways to change. Chapter 4, then, is a short introduction to language usage for doing very brief therapy (NLP Meta-model of language is discussed in Chapter 15). Since hypnosis can be a powerful adjunct to therapeutic work, Chapter 5 recounts the ways in which hypnosis can be used expectationally for change work. Recall that any procedure that asks a client to go "inside" involves some level of trance.

The solution-oriented approaches developed by Steve de Shazer and his associates are quite useful for rapid change work. The "miracle question" and its variants are effective. This is covered in Chapter 6. Bill O'Hanlon's approaches are discussed in Chapter 7, and they include his "brief, respectful approaches", inclusive therapy and hypnotic work.

Derks's Social Panorama work can be effective in interesting ways by incorporating the client's images about their social environment. This is presented in Chapter 8. Milton H. Erickson was a pioneer in the area of very brief therapy. His Utilization Principle is a guideline for involving who the client is in organizing a session. The client is central to a session, and it has been said of Erickson that he devised a new approach to fit each client. Chapter 9 discusses Erickson's methods of working briefly, although, if you study his cases you will find that he was flexible in the number of sessions for any given client. Erickson's sessions were also open-ended.

Two approaches derived from Erickson's work, and then extensively developed further, are "Ordeal Therapy" as practiced by Jay Haley (Chapter 10), and "Ambiguous Function Assignments" as systematized by the Lanktons (Chapter 11). Burns has developed an approach that involves interaction with Nature, and which he calls "Nature-Guided Therapy" or "Ecotherapy". This is covered in Chapter 12.

Metaphoric approaches have been used in many ways by many practitioners. Erickson was a master of metaphor. In addition to discussing classical metaphoric work, Chapter 13 provides information on R. R. Kopp's "Metaphor Therapy", and Battino's "Guided Metaphor".

Over the years, E. L. Rossi has developed a number of rapid methods for doing therapy. He describes some of them as "fail-safe", others as polarity approaches, and is a master on minimalism in working with a client. Rossi's work is described in Chapter 14.

Neurolinguistic Programming (NLP) has been prolific in developing many ways of doing brief therapy. Some of these methods will be described in Chapter 15. "Narrative Therapy" as developed by Epston and White has the client's life story and the client as central to change work. The principles and practice of their work is the subject of Chapter 16. Rituals and ceremonies are discussed in Chapter 17.

Finally, there are some "when all else fails" comments by way of summary in Chapter 18. At the core of the author's way of doing very brief therapy is his *expectation* that it is possible and practical and learnable. Why not?

Chapter 1
Introduction to Very Brief Therapy

1.1 Introduction

My introduction to brief therapy came from examining the litera-ture on the subject a number of years ago. I was intrigued by finding a book that was enthusiastic about brief therapy being con-ducted in one year (rather than five or more), and in under fifty ses-sions (rather than hundreds). The book, of course, was psychody-namically oriented. In recent times, "brief" has come to mean some-thing like six to twelve sessions, much of this mandated by man-aged care systems. In fact, many of these managed care systems will tie a number of sessions to a particular diagnosis. This is carrying the intrusion of the medical model into psychotherapy to what I consider to be ridiculous extremes, so I am being explicit about this at the outset of this book. The medical model works well when prescribing a particular drug for a specific infection for a set number of days. But people who seek the help of psychotherapists are not diseased, they are troubled and stuck and seek some guidance for their unique concerns. A diagnosis such as "depres-sion" is manifested uniquely by each person, and their individual-ity and history must be taken into account in any work done with them. It is in this sense that Milton H. Erickson's *Utilization Principle* is primary in determining how you work with a client. This prin-ciple simply states that every client is absolutely unique, and that the treatment needs to be specific to that client (and not some abstract diagnosis). The client's uniqueness is *utilized* in working *with* them.

I came to the central theme of this book via something I heard Steve de Shazer report in one of his presentations. This was about the results of a study they carried out at the Brief Therapy Family Center of Milwaukee. The receptionist was told to randomly tell each new client, after looking at their intake form, that their particular concern usually took five *or* ten sessions. The center's staff did not know what the client was told. Later analysis showed that the five session clients started doing significant work around the fourth session, and that the ten session clients started doing significant work around the eighth or ninth session. In essence, the clients were told when to *expect* change to begin, and they responded appropriately. My reasoning then was, why wait for the fourth or eighth session, why not have the expectation be that significant work can be done in the first session and, further, why not imply that *one* session was all that was usually necessary? So, that is what I do. *Very brief therapy* to me means that I rarely see clients more than once or twice, with one being the most frequent number of sessions. Of course, I tell each client that I will see them for as many sessions as they feel are helpful.

The essence of what will be the content of this book is how to use *expectation* in psychotherapy. In a sense, this is akin to the placebo effect, and there is much evidence on how well placebos work in a variety of areas. This chapter introduces a number of related concepts and research. In particular, the work of Wampold, Hubble, Duncan, S. D. Miller and others is discussed in some detail as it directly impacts on the nature of psychotherapy and how it is practiced. In this book I am presenting how I work in the field. Are my methods and my approach significantly better than the hundreds of other approaches out there? Is any one approach better than any other? Why bother reading this book, especially when you are already certain that what you do is *the* best way to do this work? After all, I am eclectic and pragmatic in how I work—if what I am doing is not working, then I switch to something else. I do have a bunch of preferred things that I do, and I do generally function out of an Ericksonian perspective. These preferred methods are described in the remainder of this book, yet they are presented so that you can read about many different ways of operating effectively and efficiently. What about the research evidence supporting how I work? In effect, I have personally done no research on this subject—as in many books, the evidence is anecdotal, i.e., I really do see my clients only one or two times. Since I do have a background as a "hard" scientist (I have spent most of my adult professional life as a professor of chemistry, and I am still actively functioning in that capacity), it is incumbent upon me to present some research in the field. Therefore, I am going to do that in this chapter by first citing (in the next section) the work of a qualified academic researcher (B. E. Wampold). This is followed by a description of the ongoing research being carried out by B. L. Duncan and S. D. Miller and colleagues. Finally, the seminal work of Talmon on single session therapy is discussed. It is my hope that the remainder of the book proves useful to you.

1.2 The Great Psychotherapy Debate

This is the title of Wampold's book (2001) summarizing an enormous amount of research on psychotherapy. This book is a solid example of a scholar at work, and it is replete with relevant references—the interested reader is urged to consult them. This section sets the stage for the rest of this book to whet the reader's appetite. At the outset, Wampold (p. 2) states, "The pressures of the health care delivery system have molded psychotherapy to resemble medical treatments." Then, he states categorically (p. 2), "In this book, the scientific evidence will be presented that shows that psychotherapy is incompatible with the medical model and that conceptualizing psychotherapy in this way distorts the name of the endeavor." To start off, he offers the following working definition of psychotherapy (p. 3):

> Psychotherapy is a primarily interpersonal treatment that is based on psychological principles and involves a trained therapist and a client who has a mental disorder, problem, or complaint; it is intended by the therapist to be remedial for the client's disorder, problem, or complaint; and it is adapted or individualized for the particular client and his or her disorder, problem, or complaint.

Wampold contrasts the medical model with the contextual model. They are both summarized here before continuing with describing his results (see pp. 13–20).

1.2.1 Five Components of the Medical Model

1. As the first component of the medical model of psychotherapy, a client is conceptualized to have a disorder, problem, or

complaint. *DSM-IV* (American Psychiatric Association, 1994) is one way of categorizing (mental) disorders, but these diagnoses are not necessary for the application of the medical model to psychotherapy.

2. For the second component, a psychological explanation for the client's disorder, problem, or complaint is proposed. Since there are many approaches to psychotherapy, there are also many alternative explanations for a given disorder. This is generally not the case for medical disorders.

3. In the medical model of psychotherapy, it is stipulated that each psychotherapeutic approach incorporate a mechanism of change. That is, each theory or approach of psychotherapy implicitly or explicitly involves a mechanism, such as making the unconscious conscious in psychodynamic approaches.

4. There are specific therapeutic actions prescribed, often in treatment manuals. That is, a diagnosis of X requires a treatment of Y.

5. With regard to *specificity*, which is the critical aspect of the medical model, there is an implication that there are specific therapeutic ingredients which are remedial for a particular disorder, problem or complaint.

The medical model has, of course, worked quite well for medical problems. Yet, impressing that model with its *empirically supported treatments* (ESTs) and its *diagnostically related groups* (DRGs) into the radically different situation of psychotherapy requires a leap of faith worthy of the most fundamentalist religions.

With respect to the *contextual model*, Wampold writes (p. 27):

> The contextual model states that the treatment procedures used are beneficial to the client because of the *meaning* attributed to those procedures rather than because of their specific psychological effects. [Emphasis added.]

That is, in this model it is the common contextual factors that are emphasized. Wampold cites Frank and Frank (1991) with respect to the components shared by all approaches to psychotherapy:

1. Psychotherapy involves an emotionally charged, confiding relationship with a helping person (the therapist).

2. There is a healing setting in which the client talks to a helping professional the client believes can help him or her.

3. There exists a rationale, a conceptual scheme, or a myth that provides a plausible explanation for the client's symptoms, and also provides a ritual or procedure for resolving them. In this wise, the client must believe in the treatment, or be led to believe in it. [RB comment: this involves an element of the placebo effect.]

Wampold then cites (p. 25) six elements discussed by Frank and Frank (1991) as being common to the rituals and procedures used by all psychotherapists:

> *First*, the therapist combats the client's sense of alienation by developing a relationship that is maintained after the client divulges feelings of demoralization. *Second*, the therapist maintains the client's expectation of being helped by linking hope for improvement to the process of therapy. *Third*, the therapist provides new learning experiences. *Fourth*, the client's emotions are aroused as a result of the therapy. *Fifth*, the therapist enhances the client's sense of mastery or self-efficacy. *Sixth*, the therapist provides opportunities for practice.

A basic question that has been studied for decades is: "Does psychotherapy work?" That is, is it effective in helping clients? Grissom (1996) reviewed 68 meta-analyses that had collected results from studies comparing psychotherapies with no-treatment controls. He found an aggregate effect size of 0.75 for the efficacy of psychotherapy. Other similar studies over the years have shown an effect size in the range of 0.75 to 0.85. This means that the average client receiving psychotherapy is better off than about 80% of untreated clients. A reasonable conclusion from these studies is that psychotherapy is remarkably efficacious in helping clients. This result does not support, of course, either the contextual model or the medical model, but it is comforting to know that psychotherapy is useful.

The next question with regard to psychotherapy has to do with *relative efficacy*, i.e., are there some approaches that are clearly more efficacious than others? The partisans (or believers) in particular therapies and, specifically, the developers of those therapies, have long been vociferous in the advantages of their "psychotheology" (to cite a word promulgated by the developers of NLP, R. Bandler and J. Grinder) over all other psychotheologies. Rather than simply promote and describe another useful way of doing therapy, a "new" therapy is sold as if it were the best or, at least, better than all of the others. Does the research literature support such statements? Wampold writes about this as follows (2001, p. 72):

> The uniform efficacy of psychotherapies was emphasized in the subtitle of Rosenzweig's article by reference to the Dodo bird's conclusion at the end of the caucus race in *Alice in Wonderland*: "At last the Dodo said, Everybody has won, and all must have prizes" (Rosenzweig, 1936, p. 412). Since that time, uniform efficacy, which has been referred to as the Dodo bird effect, has been considered empirical support for those who believe that common factors are the efficacious aspect of psychotherapy.

In his Chapter 4 entitled "Relative Efficacy: The Dodo Bird Was Smarter Than We Have Been Led to Believe" (2001, pp. 72–118), Wampold cites study after study and meta-analysis after meta-analysis about efficacy to conclude (2001, p. 118): "The lack of differences among a variety of treatments casts doubt on the hypothesis that specific ingredients are responsible for the benefits of psychotherapy." To be specific about two diagnoses (2001, p. 115), Wampold states: "As was the case for depression, there is no convincing evidence that one treatment for anxiety disorder is superior to another treatment."

In searching for *specific effects*, Wampold draws the conclusion (2001, p. 147): "The results of the studies using component designs, placebo control groups, mediating constructs, and moderating constructs consistently failed to find evidence for specificity." In examining the *therapeutic alliance*, Wampold's conclusions are (2001, p. 158):

> Examination of a single common factor, the working alliance, convincingly demonstrated that this factor is a key component of psychotherapy. ... However, it appears that the relationship accounts for dramatically more of the variability in outcomes than does the totality of specific ingredients.

In his Chapter 7 (2001, pp. 159–183), Wampold considers the factors of allegiance to a treatment approach and adherence to its respective protocol and concludes (2001, p. 183):

> In a critical test of the contextual model versus the medical model, examination of allegiance and adherence provides strong support for the contextual model. ... When the therapist believes that the treatment is efficacious, he or she will enthusiastically communicate that belief to the client. Adherence to treatment protocols was generally not associated with outcomes, although a few notable exceptions were found.

Continuing, with respect to therapists, Wampold states (2001, p. 202):

> The essence of therapy is embodied in the therapist. ... Clearly, the person of the therapist is a critical factor in the success of therapy. ... *The evidence is clear that the type of treatment is irrelevant, and adherence to protocol is misguided, but yet the therapist, within each of the treatments, makes a tremendous difference.* [Emphasis added.]

Wampold makes eleven recommendations based on his findings. His Recommendation 5 (2001, p. 225) simply states: "Abolish the EST movement as presently conceptualized." (EST refers to the Empirically Supported Treatment movement which Wampold's book clearly shows to *not* be supported by the research data.)

Lambert (1992) gives a chart presented by Wampold (2001, p. 208) that summarizes Lambert's findings with respect to the percentage of improvement in psychotherapy patients as a function of therapeutic factors. The largest contributor (40%) is extratherapeutic change, or those factors that are part of the client or their environment that aid in recovery regardless of participation in therapy. Common factors—common things found in most therapies such as empathy, warmth, acceptance, encouragement of risk taking etc.—contribute 30%. Techniques which are unique to specific therapies contribute 15%; and expectancy (or the placebo effect) also contributes 15%. With respect to Wampold's Recommendation 5, it is apparent that his justification for this recommendation is Lambert's assigning only 15% to technique.

Wampold's contribution to "the great psychotherapy debate" is of major significance.

1.3 The Heart and Soul of Change

Before discussing the contributions in *The Heroic Client* (next section), a number of relevant items will be presented from a volume edited by Hubble, Duncan and Miller (1999) entitled *The Heart & Soul of Change: What Works in Therapy*. This book has many contributors and summarizes much research in the field. Chapter 4 in this book (pp. 91–131) by Tallman and Bohart is about the client as a common factor: clients as self-healers. Since it makes sense to simply quote relevant passages from this chapter, they follow with page citations:

> Our thesis in this chapter is that the client's capacity for self-healing is the most important common factor in psychotherapy. ... Therapy facilitates naturally occurring healing aspects of clients' lives. Therapists function as support systems and resource providers. ... In this chapter we argue that the most parsimonious explanation for the dodo bird verdict is that it is the client, not the therapist or technique, that makes therapy work. [P. 91.]

> The data point to the inevitable conclusion that the primary agent of change, the "engine" of change, is the client. [P. 98.]

> We contend (a) it is client self-healing that best accounts for the dodo bird verdict, (b) placebos work by activating clients' agency, and (c) the therapeutic relationship is a resource that clients use like any other, and clients contribute most to that factor as well. [P. 103.]

> The evidence supports our view of the client's active investment in the change process. Clients are not merely conduits or "processors" of information. Instead they are active thinkers who are continually generative and creative in every day life. They modify old concepts and use them, create new concepts, think of alternatives, derive rules and implications. In therapy they are active agents, creatively working to get from the therapist what they want and

need, protecting themselves when necessary, and actively supporting the therapist when they think the therapist needs it. Compatible with this view of the client, clients regard therapy as a place where they can focus on themselves, and value relational aspects over technological aspects. [P. 110.]

Therapists empathically listen, are nonjudgmental, and allow clients to tell their story. There is evidence to suggest that no matter what the therapeutic orientation, clients feel that this is the most basic and helpful thing therapists have to offer. [P. 116.]

Tallman and Bohart's chapter, of course, is backed up by many references.

For this book, Chapter 6 by Snyder, Michael and Cheavens (pp. 179–200) is of particular interest as it deals with the common factors of placebos and expectancies. These authors define *hope* in terms of two goals as follows (pp. 180–181):

Hope may be understood in terms of how people think about goals. Thinking about goals is defined in two components. First, there are the thoughts that persons have about their ability to produce one or more workable routes to their goals. And second, there are the thoughts that people have regarding their ability to begin and continue movement on selected pathways toward those goals. These two components are known respectively as *pathways thinking* and *agency thinking*. Both types of thinking must be present for a person to experience hope. ... In this model of hope, stress, negative emotions, and difficulties in coping are considered a result of being unable to envision a pathway or make movement toward a desired goal.

A series of relevant citations follow:

Therapists must have hope that the client can change. Indeed, research demonstrates the critical role of helpers' hope in enabling clients to change. [P. 182.]

In particular, settings that send the message—implicitly or explicitly—that the client can expect successful change increase the opportunity for critical agency and pathways thinking. [P. 182.]

> Research shows that successful treatment depends, at least in part, on the plausibility of a particular school's theory to the client. ... [The] therapists' confidence and mastery of a chosen method ultimately works by enhancing the client's belief in the potential of healing. ... In general, the therapeutic relationship and setting in which treatment occurs foster agency thinking (e.g., "I *can* do it"), whereas the particular rationale and therapeutic ritual act to enhance pathways thinking (e.g., "Here's *how* I can do it"). [P. 183.]

> In a series of studies, researchers have even found that 40% to 66% of clients reported positive, treatment-related improvement before attending their first session. (See Weiner-Davis, de Shazer, and Gingerich (1987), for example). [P. 183.]

> To date, studies suggest that 56% to 71% of the variance related to client change can be accounted for by change occurring in the early stages of treatment. [P. 184.]

> Frank and Frank (1991) argued that the effectiveness of placebos results from their ability to mobilize clients' expectancies for improvement. Research has provided support for this idea. Studies have found, for example, that the degree of improvement correlates positively and significantly with such expectancies (Friedman, 1963; Goldstein, 1960). [P. 186.]

> Hope therapy, in many instances, merely involves careful detective work with one's clients into what it is they really desire. [P. 190.]

Again, it should be pointed out that the materials in this chapter are well-documented.

Chapter 10 (pp. 297–328) deals with common psychosocial factors in psychiatric drug therapy, and is by R. P. Greenberg. Comments on psychiatric drug therapy are significant since there is a push by the American Psychological Association to obtain drug prescribing privileges for psychologists. Again, here are some relevant citations from this chapter:

> Over time, we have uncovered more than 30 studies addressing this issue—most often by asking participants to guess whether a drug or placebo was administered—and more than 90% of them show the double-blind was penetrated. [P. 312.]

The material in this chapter documents that effects of psychiatric drugs are inextricably bound up with psychosocial forces. ... Furthermore, with proper controls, differences in outcome between active drug and placebo have been shown to recede in treatments of depression, anxiety, and even schizophrenia. In fact, psychosocial factors are arguably the largest therapeutic component in most effective psychiatric medication treatments—more critical than dosage or blood levels of the ingested drug. [P. 315.]

Regardless of practical considerations, research findings have not invalidated the usefulness of psychiatric drugs. Findings have, however, raised questions about the magnitude of effectiveness beyond appropriately constructed placebo comparison groups. [P. 316.]

Effectiveness is optimized when patients are truly convinced that they are receiving a potent agent (one producing body sensations) from a confident practitioner who expects a successful outcome. The presentation should include an outline of the benefits to be expected, along with a description of potential side effects framed as routine indicators of the drug's power. [P. 317.]

This last citation speaks strongly to the power of expectation.

In the last chapter of the book (Chapter 14), the editors comment on the individual contributions and direct attention to what works (pp. 407–447). Here are some of their summarizing statements:

Similarly, Jerome Frank (1995, p. 91) concluded, "I'm inclined to entertain the notion that the relative efficacy of most psychotherapeutic methods depends almost exclusively on how successfully the therapist is able to make the methods fit the client's expectations."

The credibility of a given procedure, and therefore the positive expectancy effects, is enhanced when complementary to the clients' preexisting beliefs about their problems and the change process. [P. 429.]

Within the client is a theory of change waiting for discovery, a framework for intervention to be unfolded and accommodated for a successful outcome. Each client presents the therapist with a new theory to learn, a new language to practice, and new interventions to suggest. Psychotherapy, then, is an idiosyncratic, process-determined synthesis of ideas that culminates in a new theory with explanatory and predictive validity for the client's specific circumstance.

To learn the client's theory, therapists may be best served by viewing themselves as "aliens" or visitors seeking a pristine understanding of a close encounter with the clients' unique interpretations and cultural experiences. To learn clients' theories, clinicians must adopt clients' views in their terms with a very strong bias in their favor. The process begins by listening closely to the client's language. [P. 431.]

To help in this endeavor the authors list three questions (p. 432):

- What ideas do you have about what needs to happen for improvement to occur?

- Many times people have a pretty good hunch about not only what is causing a problem, but also what will resolve it. Do you have a theory of how change is going to happen here?

- In what ways do you see me and this process being helpful to attaining your goals?

Exploration for and discovery of the client's theory is a co-evolutionary process; a crisscrossing of ideas that generates a seamless connection of socially constructed meanings. The degree and intensity of our input may vary and are driven by the client's expectations of our role. [Pp. 432–3.]

1.4 Duncan, Miller and Sparks's "Heroic Client"

Barry L. Duncan and Scott D. Miller and their colleagues have done much research on the effectiveness of psychotherapy and the factors contributing to it. In a way this has culminated in *The Heroic Client* by Duncan, Miller and Sparks (2004). The subtitle of this book is *A Revolutionary Way to Improve Effectiveness Through Client–Directed, Outcome–Informed Therapy*. This is a revised and expanded edition of Duncan and Miller's earlier book (2000). This book continues many of the arguments put forward by

Wampold (2001) reported above about the medical model versus the contextual model. In Chapter 1, Duncan, Miller and Sparks make two interesting observations:

> Data from over forty years of increasingly sophisticated research shows little support for
>
> • The utility of psychiatric diagnosis in either selecting the course or predicting the outcome of therapy (the myth of diagnosis).
>
> • The superiority of any therapeutic approach over any other (the myth of the silver-bullet cure).
>
> • The superiority of pharmacological treatment fo emotional complaints (the myth of the magic pill). [P. 9.]
>
> For example, although most would say their clinical ability has improved with experience, a sizeable body of research finds little or no relationship between the experience level and effectiveness of therapists (Clement, 1994). If anything, the data indicate that increasing the amount and type of training and experience that most therapists receive may lessen therapeutic effectiveness (Lambert and Ogles, 2004). [P. 14.]

In Chapter 2 on the myth of the medical model (pp. 21–48), these authors make the following useful comments:

> … not one major study has replicated the field trials or shown that regular mental health professionals can routinely use the *DSM* with high reliability (Kutchins and Kirk, 1997). [P. 25.]
>
> Diagnoses do not help in treatment plan or selection. … There is no correlation between diagnosis and outcome nor between diagnosis and length of treatment (Brown et al., 1999; Beutler and Clarkin, 1990). Bottom line: there are no diagnostic-specific benefits to psychotherapy. Diagnoses lack validity (Garfield, 1986). In mental health, naming a problem with a diagnostic moniker neither explains nor solves it. [P. 26.]
>
> Diagnoses brand people with labels that carry blame, hopelessness, and helplessness. … Once a label has been attached, it sticks

like glue. ... A diagnosis, once set in motion, creates an expectancy of hard going or poor outcome that is surprisingly resilient (Salovey and Turk, 1991). Left unchecked, the expectation becomes the person. Should this occur, observers (nonprofessionals and clinicians alike) unwittingly distort information to conform to their expectations. [P. 27.]

Clients accept diagnosis as a medical fact and become enslaved by its implications. [P. 28.)]

... the *DSM* transforms ordinary reactions to life stress to billable pathology. [P. 29.]

A diagnosis describes only individual behavior; it ignores relational, environmental, and cultural influences. [Pp. 29–30.]

One of the central themes of the heroic client book is becoming client-directed. Chapter 3 (pp. 49–80) is devoted to this subject, and here are some useful comments:

Clients' heroic stories pave the way for change. Mental health professionals can also incorporate the heroic aspects of clients' lives by enlisting their resources from the world outside therapy. ...Whatever path the therapist takes, it is important to remember that the purpose is to identify not what the clients need but what they already have that they can put to use in reaching their goals. [P. 55.]

To develop a change–focus, a therapist can listen for and validate change for the better, whenever and for whatever reason it occurs. [P. 56.]

Regardless of how they sound, we accept client's goals at face value because those are the desires that will excite and motivate the client to initiate action on his or her own behalf. [P. 69.]

... counselors allow the client's view of change to direct therapeutic choices. [P. 72.]

A second theme has to do with becoming outcome-informed, and this is the subject of Chapter 4 (pp. 81–118).

Howard, Kopte, Krause, and Orlinsky (1986) found that between 60 and 65 percent of people experienced significant symptomatic relief within one to seven visits—figures that increased to 70–75 percent after six months, and 85 percent at one year. [P. 83.]

Brown et al. (1999) found that therapeutic relationships in which no improvement occurred by the third visit did not on the average result in improvement over the entire course of treatment. [P. 85.]

... feedback from clients is essential and even improves success. [P. 85.]

1.4.1 The Outcome Rating Scale

Miller and Duncan (2000) have developed an outcome rating scale (ORS) which is administered at the beginning of the session. This is available on-line at www.talkingcure.com for a free download. This instrument takes about one minute for the client to fill out. It is reproduced on the next page.

Each line is adjusted to be 10 cm long so that by measuring with a cm ruler the client can measure to the nearest centimeter. This gives a total score of 40. Miller and Duncan found that a score of 25 was the clinical cut-off, i.e., persons scoring over 25 typically represented scores of persons not in therapy. This means that the therapist can determine at the beginning of the session the client's current feelings.

1.4.2 The Session Rating Scale

The second instrument is the session rating scale (SRS) and this is administered towards the end of the session. It is similar to the ORS and is reproduced on page 17.

Outcome Rating Scale (ORS)

Name: _____   Age (yrs):_____

ID# _____   Sex: M/F _____

Session # _____   Date: _____

Looking back over the last week, including today, help us under-stand how you have been feeling by rating how well you have been doing in the following areas of your life, where marks on the left represent low levels and marks on the right indicate high levels.

Individually
(Personal wellbeing)

....

Interpersonally
(Family, close relationships)

....

Socially
(Work, school, friendships)

....

Overall
(General sense of wellbeing)

....

Institute for the Study of Therapeutic Change
www.talkingcure.com

© 2000, Scott D. Miller and Barry L. Duncan

Session Rating Scale (SRS V.3.0)

Name: _____   Age (yrs):_____

ID# _____   Sex: M/F _____

Session # _____   Date: _____

Please rate today's session by placing a hash mark on the line nearest to the description that best fits your experience.

Relationship

....

I did not feel heard, understood,   I felt heard, understood,
and respected.   and respected.

Goals and Topics

....

We did not work on or talk about what I   We worked on and talked about what
wanted to work on and talk about.   I wanted to work on and talk about.

Approach or Method

....

The therapist's approach is not   The therapist's approach
a good fit for me.   is a good fit for me.

Overall

....

There was something missing in   Overall, today's session was
the session today.   right for me.

Institute for the Study of Therapeutic Change
www.talkingcure.com

© 2000, Lynn D. Johnson, Scott D. Miller and Barry L. Duncan

With respect to the use of these two scales, the authors state (p. 91):

> In addition to assessing factors that research has linked to positive outcomes, the SRS is highly feasible. Like the ORS, the instrument takes less than a minute to administer and score. Furthermore, the content of the items makes sense to both clients and therapists, giving the scale good face validity. The SRS is scored similarly to the ORS, by adding the total of the client's marks on the 10-centimeter lines.
>
> Using the ORS and the SRS in concert represents the only feasible measurement system available that tracks both outcome *and* process, thereby taking advantage of the two known predictors of outcome.

Also, all scoring and interpretation of these measures is done together *with* clients. This procedure gives the therapist direct and rapid information about what is going on with the client at the beginning and end of each session. Both instruments are used to decide on what to do during the session and in the future. Rather than rely on "gut" feelings or the therapist's intuition, observation, and interpretation, the client provides direct feedback in a timely fashion. The authors provide additional information about the use of these instruments in practice. It is to be hoped that all therapists will adopt and use these free assessment instruments.

In Chapter 5 on the client's theory of change, the authors emphasize that it is the client's theory about how change will come about for them that is the important element. It is interesting that they refer to what they do with clients as "conversing" or "conversation," rather than interviewing. A conversation is collaborative and respectful, while an interview is a one-up/one-down situation. Later in this book we will describe the Guided Metaphor approach which is built around the client's own life story. In this regard (p. 123), the authors state, "… clients are novelists who carefully choose words to convey their story in a specific light." On p. 127, the authors write about having abandoned the "killer" *Ds* of diagnosis, disorders, dysfunction, disease, disabilities, and deficit. At least linguistically, this is an excellent choice and it gets away from the problems of labeling. At the end of this chapter the authors have two simple statements (p. 146), "… clients have taught us to use their map as the best guide to the therapeutic territory." and "As a field, we should de-emphasize our theories and instead focus on those of our clients."

"The Myth of the Magic Pill: The Ethics and Science of Medication" is the subject of Chapter 6 (pp. 147–77). Duncan, Miller, and Sparks with help from G. Jackson, R. P. Greenberg, and K. Kinchin explore the myths surrounding psychoactive medications, and present four flaws of drug research:

> *Flaw Number One:* Client Versus Clinician Ratings. "They found that both old and new antidepressants showed an advantage of about 20 percent over the placebo on clinician-rated measures, but *no advantage* on client-rated measures." [P. 152.]

> *Flaw Number Two:* Compromised Blind. "Greenberg and Fisher (1997) note that the use of inert sugar pills as the placebo in the vast majority of studies actually makes it possible for most participants and clinicians to tell who is getting the real drug and who isn't." [P. 153.] [In a Prozac study, clinicians accurately predicted medication for responders (87%) and placebo for nonresponders (74%). This is quite remarkable.]

> *Flaw Number Three:* Time of Measurement. [Clinical trials are rarely run for long enough time periods.]

> *Flaw Number Four:* Conflicts of Interest. [This is to report accurately who is funding the study and with whom the authors are affiliated. Too often the funders are the drug companies themselves, and the researchers are affiliated in some way with the company.]

Here are a smattering of further insightful statements:

> The problem with these common beliefs and practices emerges, however, when we examine them in the light of research. Empirically, there is little support for:

> - The ubiquitous biochemical imbalance.

> - The superior effectiveness of drug treatment.

> - Better outcomes when therapy is combined with drugs. [P. 165.]

Despite fifty years of research, the invention of electron microscopy, the advent of radiolabeling techniques, the revolution of molecular biology, and the merger of computers with neuroimaging machines, no reliable biological marker has ever emerged as the definitive cause of any psychiatric "disease." What many fail to appreciate is that biochemical imbalances and other so-called functional mind diseases remain the only territory in medicine where diagnoses are permitted without a single confirmatory test of underlying pathology. [P. 167.]

[With respect to the newer SSRI antidepressants] ... the drug out-performed placebo pills by only 18 percent. ... The greater number of side effects participants experienced, the better the outcome was judged by both clients and clinicians. [P. 171.]

To sum up, research evidence indicates that for most experiences of depression, combination treatments [i.e., drug plus psychother-apy] do not provide added benefits and may unnecessarily subject clients to unpleasant side effects and extra costs. [P. 175.]

This is quite an indictment of the medical model as manifested in drug therapies.

Summarizing, the work of Duncan and Miller and colleagues provides a sound basis for seriously considering operating as a psychotherapist through client–directed and outcome–informed therapy, and to use their feedback forms in your sessions. This may be hopeful thinking, but I choose to consider their research and recommendations as being supportive of making the thesis of this book in terms of very brief therapy being both possible and practical.

1.5 Moshe Talmon's Single Session Therapy (SST)

Talmon (1990) worked in a large health maintenance organization in California and did the interesting study of examining how many psychotherapy sessions clients attended. He found three rather sur-prising things in his study: (1) the modal or most frequent length of therapy for every one of the therapists was a single session; (2) 30 per cent of all patients chose to come for only one session in a period of one year; and (3) there was essentially no correlation in a follow-up study between what the client stated helped them, and what the therapist thought was helpful in that single session. Quoting Talmon (1990, p. 111),

> ... in most of the SST cases where patients reported particularly successful outcomes, the therapist appeared to have conducted a rather simple, almost dull session. In fact, in many successful SSTs, it is the patient who appears in control and sets the pace for change.

(Please note that Talmon made this observation more than a decade before *The Heroic Client* was published! See previous section.) In his introductory chapter, Talmon makes the interesting observation that the "founder" of single-session therapy was probably Sigmund Freud who treated a number of his patients in one session, the most famous case being curing Gustav Mahler of his impotence during a single long walk in the woods! (Of course, psychoanalytic treatment grew longer and longer ...) Talmon's book contains many case studies, and a systematic presentation of how to do single session therapy. In what follows I highlight some of his findings.

There were more no-shows in patients who were provided immediate appointments, in contrast with those who had to wait. In fact, a study by Weiner-Davis, de Shazer and Gingerich (1987) showed that when clients were asked about beneficial or useful changes that had occurred between the time they made their appointment and the appointment, that most clients reported useful changes. The therapist's task is simply to elicit these changes by asking about them (if you do not ask, clients generally do not volunteer this information). It is important at the end of the session (see SRS above) to air last-minute issues by asking about them. In giving final feedback, Talmon suggests doing the following four things (pp. 50–1):

> *Acknowledgment.* Regardless of how much the therapist and the patient have accomplished in a single session, it is important to acknowledge the reason that brought the patient to the session.

Compliments. The therapist should underline what has been learned about the patient's thinking, affect, and behavior that is useful in solving the problem.

Diagnosis. Diagnosis (or assessment) is often presented not as a *DSM-III-R* label but rather as a reframing of the problem in solvable or autonomous terms.

Prescription (or Task). While therapists may entertain various fancy interpretations or solutions, in SST it is most useful to present patients with the smallest and simplest task that the therapist can come up with, worded to correspond with the patient's idiosyncrasies and world view.

In a chapter on empowering patients, Talmon made some useful observations:

Yet it is undeniable that a considerable number of patients are capable of recovering "against all odds" in ways that are very difficult to explain using plausible and logical thinking within traditional theories. [P. 65.]

Talmon (1990, p. 66) cites Pelletier (1977, 1978) who found five characteristics common to all patients who recovered despite great odds. These characteristics which apply to both physical and mental problems follow:

- Profound intrapsychic change through meditation, prayer, or other spiritual practice.

- Profound interpersonal changes, placing the patient's relationships with others on a more solid footing.

- Alterations in diet. These patients no longer took their food for granted.

- A deep sense of the spiritual as well as material aspects of life.

- A feeling that their recovery was not a gift or spontaneous remission but rather a long, hard struggle that they had won themselves.

Two more comments are particularly relevant to this book.

There is a clear discrepancy between what most therapists see as an appropriate length of therapy (often described as a matter of years) and the average length of therapy in reality (from four to six sessions). Furthermore, not many therapists negotiate the expected length of treatment with their patients. They often view therapy as an open-ended process. [P. 99.]

Viewing each and every session as a whole, complete in itself, can serve as an alternative attitude not only toward SST but toward each and every session of psychotherapy. [P. 117.]

Talmon was a pioneer in bringing out in the open much that had been already going on in terms of very brief therapy, and his book contains much useful guidance for working in this manner.

1.6 Some Concluding Comments

When I outlined this chapter, I had not yet read the books by Wampold, Duncan, Miller and colleagues, and I thought it was going to be much simpler. Yet, after reading their books (which have been outlined in this chapter), I felt it was necessary to include them here to set the stage for what follows. After another introductory style chapter on expectation and as-if, two brief chapters on rapport and language for very brief therapy, the remainder of the book describes—chapter by chapter—the various things that I might do in a given session. Again, since my sessions are not time-limited, it is not unusual for me to utilize several interventions from seemingly disparate approaches. If what you are doing is not working, then do something else. If what you are doing is working, then do more of it *and* connected variations. *Before* reaching the point of "if all else fails," ask the client what works for them, and involve the client in their therapy. After all, they do know themselves better than you ever will.

Am I being simplistic in promulgating very brief therapy? Perhaps. I do see some clients several times, and some come back to see me at long intervals for a "tune-up" or with new concerns. Yet *my* expectation is invariably: this is the last session we will need.

Chapter 2
Expectation and As-If

2.1 Importance of Expectation, Motivation and As-If

Expectation has to do with the future—anticipation of what it is that is going to happen soon. There are long-range expectations, of course, but I suspect that most of them are actually short-term, as in today, tomorrow or next week. Some expectations can be "great" as in the novel of that name by Charles Dickens, whilst others can be small or simple. When they make an appointment to see a therapist I believe the client's expectation is that the time spent with the therapist will be helpful in terms of resolving whatever concerns they bring to the session. For a client to be sufficiently motivated to make an appointment, there must be a significant level of frustration with being stuck, with being at an impasse, and of having tried on their own. After all, seeing a therapist involves time and money commitments, as well as the stress of exposing vulnerabilities. The common notion of visiting a therapist involves baring one's inner self, talking about private and perhaps secret matters, and a great deal of trust in the therapist's integrity, skill, honesty and confidentiality.

At some workshop I attended the trainer stated that therapists had to provide the three Ps: Protection, Permission and Power. Sometimes going to a therapist is a matter of "last hope" in the sense of, "I've tried everything else, and I was told that you might be able to help." This applies to both mental and physical concerns. When a person has exhausted the medical establishment in terms of finding out what is wrong with them, then conventional wisdom frequently states something like "It must be in your head, go see a shrink." A recent client was in this category telling me that all of the medical tests were negative, and that some of the doctors thought there might be a possibility of some incurable disease such as amyotrophic lateral sclerosis (ALS) really being the culprit—come back in six months for some more tests! So we talked about mind/body interactions and psychoneuroimmunology and working out ways to live with and cope with the stresses of this unresolved physical problem. I was providing hope and coping skills and an expectation that these things might be of benefit. I also made sure that she was not giving up on modern medicine. She was certainly motivated, and the person who referred her to me had such glowing things to say about what I did that her expectations were high, even through her healthy skepticism.

Bernie Siegel has said repeatedly, "What's wrong with hope?" Medical practitioners are cautioned in their training to avoid giving "false hope." I also trust that they are trained to *not* give true despair in terms of mentioning all of the possible terrible things that this physical concern could be. The *nocebo effect* has to do with harmful predictions being made; while the *placebo effect* has to do with positive and healthy outcomes. Once upon a time placebos were an important part of medical practice. "Take this green pill for one week." "The literature does not say much yet about this purple pill, but my patients who have taken it have gotten good results." After all, one of the most important aspects of double-blind studies is to find out how the active drug or treatment fares against a placebo. The extensive literature on placebos shows that they are frequently of comparable effectiveness as the active treatment. Yet, treatments are trumpeted and promoted when the drug in question is shown to be, say, 42% effective and the placebo is only (!) 37% effective. I am not making these numbers up. They can be found in all of those microscopically printed hand-outs that accompany drugs. In my scientific career I have studied statistics and probability theory enough to be quite suspicious of promoting a treatment on such a slim margin, but this is done all of the time.

Hope and expectation are inextricably connected. When I tell a prospective client that I rarely see people more than one or two times, the expectation is established that we will be able to do useful things together during this first and, perhaps, only session. Why drag things out? Let's do it right now. And, let's do as many things as I can think of right now. And, too, tell me what it is that you think will work for you or help you, since you are the expert on you. If you are not sure, please guess. Starting with these premises, it is no wonder that the expectation of rapid change frequently becomes its own self-fulfilling prophecy. (The prophecy of ten or more sessions is also a self-fulfilling one.) Therefore, I place *expectation* at the center of how I work, and this book is all about how to implement that expectation. Does it work with everyone? No. Is it worth testing in your own practice? Yes. If the client is sufficiently motivated to come and see you, then you can reciprocate with your motivation to see the client a minimal number of times.

At this point it is worth quoting Kay Thompson's statement in response to a rhetorical question about expectation (Kane and Olness, 2004, p. 293):

> Question: How much of my success rate do I attribute to my non-specific expectation that people can do these things?
>
> T[hompson]: Ninety-nine percent. My expectation has a great deal to do with it and they tell me that. I have worked with people who have failed to learn with other people. They say, "The difference is I know you believe." That may be corny. That's where Milton Erickson taught me to come from. This nonsense about remaining objective; remaining objective does not mean you do not care. There are those people who can remain objective and still be compassionate. And I think that's important.

2.2 The Theory of Change

Although it was published over thirty years ago, the seminal work on change by Watzlawick, Weakland and Fisch (1974) still contains many practical ideas as to how change comes about in psychotherapy and society. Their contributions will be summarized in this section. The authors characterize change as being of two types.

The first kind of change is *first-order change,* and this is characterized as *doing more of the same.* As such, this is *working within the system,* and is the most common solution used by institutions such as schools, industry, the government and the military. If a certain level of punishment, let's say, has not worked to hinder or stop a particular behavior, then the solution is to escalate that punishment. With respect to substance abuse the various "wars" on drugs have increased interdiction and penalties, and have introduced more militarization. On p. 39 of their book, the authors indicate that there are three basic ways in which mishandling results in maintaining the problem (emphasis in original):

A. A solution is attempted by denying that a problem is a problem; *action is necessary, but it is not taken.*

B. Change is attempted regarding a difficulty which for all practical purposes is either unchangeable ... or nonexistent: *action is taken when it should not be.*

C. An error in logical typing is committed and a game without end established ... *action is taken at the wrong level.*

This suggests that a first step in working with a client is to find out what solutions have already been tried so that you know what hasn't worked, and what to avoid doing more of.

The second kind of change is *second-order change* which may be considered to be *change of change*. That is, this kind of change is external to or outside of the existing system, and implies changing the system itself. Second-order change is *meta* to the system, and involves a discontinuity or logical jump: it may appear to be uncommonsensical, paradoxical, unexpected, nonsensical, weird and puzzling. The crucial question becomes "what" and not "why". With respect to governmental strategies to control the use of "illegal" drugs, stepping outside of the punishment mode and into a medical mode would be a second-order change strategy. This is, of course, the strategy on this subject that appears to be working in European countries.

With respect to this book, you might even consider the idea of working as if every session were the last one, and expecting the first session to be the only one that is needed for meaningful change to be a second-order change tactic.

2.3 The Power of As-If

Acting "as-if" is magical. It is the fantasy play of children (and adults), it is theater and play-acting, and it has the power of converting imagination into reality. If you will, as-if-ing involves faith and belief and hope and expectation. It is the essence of the placebo effect in the sense that *as the person believes* in the efficacy of the particular treatment or drug, the placebo-taker *acts as if* the placebo were the "real" curative with all of its potency and power. Thus, there are mind/body interactions involved with as-if, *and* there are mind/mind interactions as well. Acting as if the relationship with your spouse has significantly improved will change that relationship. Acting as if your life has taken a turn for the better and that you are happy affects how you think, feel, and act. Acting as if the cancer in your body is *part of you* rather than *apart from you* makes it more accessible to your immune system having an effect on it. Acting as if the chemotherapy you are receiving is a golden gift from God to heal you is healing (the converse of it being a poison administered by unfeeling technicians exacerbates side effects).

Tests that have been run on actors and actresses who act as if they are depressed, anxious, tense, happy, elated, nervous, phobic, angry etc., and people who are diagnosed with one of those labels or, let's say, observably happy, show that there are no essential differences in the biological and mental test markers for those states between those acting and those being in those states. This is remarkable, and a therapist needs to be aware of these effects.

Much of the material described separately in individual chapters later in this book is based on the power of as-if.

2.4 Reframing

Watzlawick et al.'s (1974) second-order approach of choice is reframing. One of the best examples of reframing is given by the late Kay Thompson (Kane and Olness, 2004, pp. 94–5):

How many of you can describe the physiological responses that go with the word anxiety? Everybody says, sure I can. Palms get sweaty and your heartbeat goes faster, and you get either warm or cold depending on the way you respond to stress, and you breathe faster, and you worry. That's anxiety. Would you also define for me the physiological responses that go with the word anticipation? You are anticipating going out on a date or to a conference you have been looking forward to. Your palms get a little sweaty, your heart beats faster, and your mouth gets a little dry, and you get a little cold or warm, depending on the way you do it. Isn't that what I just said about anxiety?

Anticipation is a very different kind of feeling, isn't it, than anxiety? By reframing the physiological response to anxiety into anticipation, all you are really doing is getting the individual to recognize that they have more control over their physiology, and that they can begin to look forward to something with much more anticipation that they previously would have looked at with anxiety.

While I have my Kay Thompson volume open, let me add a number of quotes that are more or less relevant to reframing:

Simply giving new information is not enough. It has to be reframed so they can make use of it, so they can utilize it. [P. 98.]

I'm offering patients the option of looking at things differently. [P. 291.]

When something happens to us that we don't like, we say, "It's not fair." That has been instilled in us. It's still in us. We need to recognize and understand and utilize that. It's not fair for you to let something that happened a long time ago in a different circumstance and in a different situation influence the response that you are going to have today or tomorrow. *It's not fair!* [P. 307.]

And so when you know that you know everything you need to know, even though some of it you didn't really know you knew; but now that you know that you don't really need to know whether you knew it, you can let yourself know everything that you need to know in order to do this, any time you know you need it. [P. 156.]

How do you frame that pain is a signal? When everything that can be done and should be done has been done, that the pain will be gone. [P. 220.]

When we are working with the patient, in talking about resistance, I think it is so important that you adopt the "Yes, but" philosophy. When the patient gives you some problem, you can agree with them, "*Yes*, it is a problem, *but*" and then you present a different perspective, one which they may not have thought of before. I think I am particularly good at that. When somebody gives me a really really significant obstacle for them, I'll say, "You know, that's really true, but I wonder whether," and I'll come up with something that will demand that they change their perspective. [P. 237.]

There are two sentences that are my philosophy about pain. ... Pain is a danger or a warning signal, period. When everything that can be done and should be done, has been done, there is no longer any reason to have the pain. [P. 267.]

You can be as miserable as you need to be, but you don't have to be painful about it. [P. 289.]

It is my belief that the placebo is effective, because it frees your body to do the things your body knows how to do, without the interference with having to worry. [P. 321.]

It's nice to know that you can remember to forget what wasn't important to remember any way, the way you know how to do that, either by forgetting to remember it, or instead by remembering to forget it, or alternatively, perhaps you'll decide somewhere inside to remember to forget to remember or to forget to remember to forget. Either way is fine, just let your mind do the work. I know you won't mind letting your mind do that. The mind knows by itself how to mind, that's right. [P. 529.]

These Kay Thompson statements are mostly about reframing when you think about them, but let's go on with some more information about the subject of reframing.

When you are constructing a reframe there are two questions to ask: "In what other context can this experience occur that would make it beneficial to this client?" and "What other meanings can be assigned to this experience that would make it beneficial?" Thus, reframes are concerned with both context and meaning or interpretation (of the content). Putting a picture into a new frame places it into a new context so that it is perceived differently. Suggesting to a client other ways of thinking about or interpreting a given event gets them to think about the event in a different way. Metaphors are a way of suggesting other ways of responding, via the content of the story or stories told. Clients are generally stuck when they have only one interpretation or can conceive of only one outcome for a given circumstance. Reframing has to do with helping a client perceive their reality differently. The art of reframing is to help the client find their own unique reframe.

2.5 *Summing Up*

In the world of as-if, reality becomes quite malleable. In the world of expectation the future and its possibilities become the present. As Kay Thompson was quoted earlier, her clients indicate that the difference is "I know you believe". It is my belief and expectation that long-term change can occur rapidly and efficiently and effectively. It is my expectation that you can have that same expectation.

Chapter 3
Rapport

3.1 Importance of Rapport

In Chapter 1, I wrote a bit about the *therapeutic alliance.* Wampold states (2001, pp. 149–50):

> The alliance between the client and the therapist is the most frequently mentioned common factor in the psychotherapy literature (Grencavage and Norcross, 1990). The concept of the alliance between therapist and client originated in the psycho-analytic tradition and was conceptualized as the healthy, affectionate, and trusting feelings toward the therapist, as differentiated from the neurotic component (i.e., transference) of the relationship. Over the years the concept of the alliance has been defined pantheoretically to include other aspects of the relationship, including (a) the client's affective relationship with the therapist, (b) the client's motivation and ability to accomplish work collaboratively with the therapist, (c) the therapist's empathic responding to and involvement with the client, and (d) client and therapist agreement about the goals and tasks of therapy.

Wampold cites three reasons for specifically marking out the therapeutic alliance as a central "common factor" in effective therapy (2001, p. 130):

> First, the alliance is mentioned prominently in the psychotherapy literature and draws attention from theorists across many disparate approaches. ... Second, there are a sufficient number of studies that have investigated the association between alliance and outcome using a variety of well-developed and accepted measures. Third, the alliance is theorized to contain a component that encompasses agreement between client and therapist on the goals and tasks of the therapy.

In his Chapter 6 (pp. 149–58) Wampold discusses the literature on alliance, and concludes (p. 158):

> Examination of a single common factor, the working alliance, convincingly demonstrated that this factor is a key component of psychotherapy. ... ... it appears that the relationship accounts for dramatically more of the variability in outcomes than does the totality of specific ingredients.

It is both important and useful for the client to feel several things during the therapeutic session.[1] First, it is important for the client to feel comfortable in your presence. "Traditional" rapport-building skills are discussed in the next section. These are ways of fitting into the client's world so that they have the sense that you understand where they come from and who they are. That is, what it is like being in their world. There needs to be a sense of collaboration, that is: *we* are in this *together*, and together can develop ways of helping you. This is not about the expert analyzing and giving advice to the client. It may have more of the feeling of a joint exploration of discovery. (Of course, you need to be sensitive to the idea that some clients want and expect a more authoritarian therapist to be there to protect them and tell them what to do. Yet, this is always there in the background since the client is coming to you as an expert.) You are helping them to help themselves and are aware that they live and function in a world outside of your office. There is then a sensitivity to the reality factors in their lives. It is crucial that your client know that you are listening to them and that their concerns have been heard. Taking notes and giving feedback and being attentive provide this assurance. (As a side note here, the most important thing you can do for people who have life-challenging diseases is simply to listen to them, to really listen, and to be there for them rather than promote your own agenda.) I want my surgeon to be a highly skilled technician, and I want my therapist to be a warm human being who knows what he or she is doing.

---

[1] I was initially going to use the word "encounter" until I realized that there are some adversarial overtones to encounter, and that "session" was essentially neutral. Comments about language usage are taken up in the next chapter.

3.2 Rapport-building Skills

This is a brief review of rapport-building skills. A more complete description of these skills can be found in Battino and South (2005, pp. 35–64) among other sources. We exist and function in the world in terms of our proprioceptive senses, and also in terms of language. We also function in many contexts, cultures, and subcultures. You generally feel more comfortable when you are with someone who shares these contexts to some degree. In fact, the closer the match to your own background, the greater the sense of rapport. There are several ways to enhance this rapport.

Pacing and leading has to do with matching certain characteristics of your client (pacing), and then subtly changing this matching (leading) in some desirable way. Perhaps the simplest example concerns walking with someone, matching their stride and pace, and then altering your pace and/or stride. Typically, and out of awareness, they will conform to the new pattern. With a client you can do this linguistically with spoken language, and physically with body language.

3.2.1 Linguistic or Verbal Pacing

There are various characteristics of speech that can be paced. Some of them are: tempo, loudness, speed, rhythm or cadence, accenting, regional or cultural accents, and breathiness. There are many ways of matching, but in general you only need to match on one characteristic for the client to feel simpatico. Also, the *pacing must be subtle*. To be effective it has to be outside of conscious awareness. If the matching is overdone, then the client will feel manipulated or mocked. Therefore, a certain amount of acting skill is required here. In effect, you want to speak your client's language so that verbally you both "fit" into the world in the same way. If a client talks very fast, you can just speed up your speech, though not necessarily to their speed. Also, you can do *cross-over pacing* by matching in another system such as finger or leg tapping.

There is some evidence that people have a preferred *representational system*, that is, their language tends to be primarily visual, physical or auditory. If you are adept at detecting this, then it makes sense to match your client's representational system by using words in that system.

3.2.2 *Physical or Postural Pacing*

In this you match your client's movements or posture or body language in some way. Again, it is only necessary to do this in one characteristic. Some examples are: head nodding; head tilting; making or not making eye contact; foot tapping; arm or leg crossing; leaning forward or back; and looking away. Perhaps the most important physical pattern to pace is that of breathing. The way you breathe is basic. You can pick up a person's breathing pattern by peripheral vision and looking at small movements in clothing, in the shoulders, or in the abdomen. (In hypnotic work it is important to pace your speech to the breathing patterns of your client.)

It is always useful for your client to feel comfortable in your presence, and that you share some ways of existing in the world.

Chapter 4
Language for Very Brief Therapy

4.1 Hypnotic Language

Since I am oriented to the use of hypnosis in most of what I do, I naturally tend to use hypnotic language forms in most everything that I do. The second edition of *Ericksonian Approaches* (Battino and South, 2005, pp. 65–144) contains a long and detailed chapter on hypnotic language forms. The interested reader should consult this book for a more comprehensive treatment than the brief one given in this chapter. A shorter version is in Battino (2000, pp. 97–116) as applied to language usage in guided imagery.

A basic tenet in the kind of hypnotic language I use is that often attributed to Milton H. Erickson, and that is the *precise use of vague language*. This means the careful and conscious choice of the exact word(s) for a particular purpose. Since the work that most therapists do is *talking* therapy, then the spoken word is the medium of change. This, of course, is not to ignore the interpersonal affective components of any session—many of which were discussed in the previous chapter. But, words are of the essence. In short, this reduces to: "What do you say after the client says something?" What you say has to be related and connected to what the client has said. If you are thinking about what you are going to say and not listening to the client, then you are not doing your job. It is not exactly counter-punching, yet there needs to be sufficient connection that the client knows you are listening to them. In this sense, the client is actually leading what is going on in the session. After all, the client is central, and not your theory of how to do therapy.

Most communication is in what linguists call *surface structures*, that is, sentences that only contain partial meaning—information is omitted. If the client says, "I am really sad," this conveys only part of the meaning. Sad about whom or what and in what way and to what depth? The *deep structure* contains the full linguistic meaning that it is possible to state. This might be something like, "I am very, very sad about my friend Jane who died yesterday—we had been close friends for many years, and this has hit me quite hard." Please note that although this sentence conveys much more about the client's emotional state, it is only a verbal communication that could be more complete, *and* it does not contain all of the internal memories and feelings associated with Jane. The word "sad" can have many interpretations, and your understanding of sadness may be quite different from that of your client. All of this may give the appearance of making communication impossible. It is difficult. *Good communication skills can be learned.* One helpful thing to keep in mind is that the *meaning of any communication is the response that you get.* So, paying attention to your client's responses is of great importance. Of course, when you are in doubt, you can always ask!

In terms of impact, some words are "more equal" than others. This section presents classes of such words. (Much is owed to NLP for this organization. Also, see Section 15.1 on the NLP Meta-model.)

A. NOMINALIZATION

When a verb or "action" word is converted into a noun or "static" word, this is a nominalization. Consider the difference between "I am depressed" or "I am in depression" versus "I wonder what is depressing me" Nominalizations seem to be cast in concrete, and when you think of yourself in nominalizations the situation appears hopeless. *Denominalization* involves converting a noun into a verb and opens the possibility of change.

B. UNSPECIFIED VERBS

No verb is completely specified in terms of an action. There are particular vague verbs that are useful with clients. Some of these are:

know, learn, understand, feel, change, wonder, do, think and fix. The listener fills in the specifics. Some examples are: "Change is easier to do than you think"; "Your body knows just how to do that."

An *unspecified referential index* is a word such as: that, how, learn, know, body etc. That is, these words do not have a specific reference. A good example is the word "it" as in, "It really will help, will it not?"

C. CAUSAL CONNECTIONS

These constructions exist in compound sentences where a connection is implied or stated between one thing and another. There are three levels of connection. The weakest is using the word "and" as in: "You are paying attention to your breathing, *and* becoming even more comfortable." The next strongest linkage uses words related to time such as: while, during, as, when and soon. "*As* you pay attention to your breathing, you are becoming more comfortable." The strongest level of causal connection uses real causal words such as: makes, causes, forces and requires. "*As* your breathing slows, it *makes* you calmer. Start these causal connections with something that is already going on such as sitting, blinking or breathing, *and* then connect that to another condition.

D. MIND-READING

This is a form of pacing and leading that involves some guesswork based on reading body language and intense conscious listening, for example, "I wonder what you are hearing/feeling/saying to yourself now."

E. LOST PERFORMATIVE

In this speech pattern *evaluative* statements are made, but it is not known who makes the statement. "It" is the favorite generalization. "It's not important just how fast you relax." "It is good, isn't it?"

F. Modal Operators of Necessity

These words *imply* particular actions and lack of choice. Here are some: will/won't, can/can't, should, have to, must, no one and necessary. "You *must* never give in/give up hope/cry/be weak/trust people ..." These words (actually, injunctions) tend to be an inheritance from our upbringing, can be part of the unfinished business or "garbage" in our lives, and can be successfully challenged.

G. Transitional Words

These are specifically words that connect or link: *and, as, while,* because, become, could, but, might, makes, may, causes, wonder, if, then, what, how, beginning, will, allow and when. The first three are italicized since they are the most useful. Generally, you start with a truism—something the person can't deny—and then bridge to an action or thought you wish to occur: "*And,* as you pay attention to your breathing, your eyes can softly close/you become more relaxed/you become calmer/your breathing softens." "*While* you pay attention to the sounds of the air conditioning, your breathing becomes deeper and more regular."

H. Meaningful Words

These words mean nothing in themselves, but are powerfully *vague* in leading people into doing inner searches. Some meaningful words are: hopes, dreams, talents, resources, sensations, memories, thoughts, beliefs, unconscious, inner mind, love, learning, loving, genuine, really, try and yet. These are wonderfully vague words and can be deliberately inserted into your speech since they allow your client to fill in the "real" meaning(s) to themselves. The word "try" is a special case since it implies *not* succeeding, and needs to be consciously used. "Just *try* harder, won't you?" Two examples of using meaningful words are: "Try doing that, now, but don't change yet." "And how much have you learned from your hopes and dreams?"

I. OR AND THE ILLUSION OF CHOICE

The word "or" presupposes the occurrence of one or more events. "You can close your eyes now *or* in a few moments." "I don't know whether you will be more relaxed now *or* in a minute or two." There *appears* to be a choice, but *some action* is presupposed.

J. AWARENESS PREDICATES

Words such as know, realize, notice, aware, find, and understand presuppose the rest of the sentence. Their use reduces to *whether* the listener is *aware* of the point you are now making. An example is: "And, you are *aware* now of *noticing* those changes." Awareness predicates bring the communication to the point of *whether* your client is *aware* of the message(s) in the sentence.

K. ADVERBS AND ADJECTIVES

These can be used to presuppose a major clause within a sentence— some choices are: deeply, readily, easily, curious, happily and simply. "Have you wondered how *easily* this happened?"

L. COMMENTARY ADVERBS AND ADJECTIVES

These are related to (k), but presuppose everything after the first word. Some good choices are: innocently, happily, luckily, necessarily, usefully, fortunately, and curiously. "*Happily*, relaxing is easy." "*Necessarily*, people do change and change is the order of life."

M. NOW

This word can be over-used, however, the *immediacy* of its meaning makes it quite potent. You may have already noticed how frequently "now" has been used in examples above. Generally, it is more effective following or preceding a pause. "And, … now … just relaxing even more."

N. THAT'S RIGHT

This was a favorite phrase of Milton H. Erickson's, and it peppered much of his trance work. "That's right, isn't it?" "That" is an ambiguous word with many possible referents—"it" can mean almost anything. "That's right, yes it is."

O. NONGRAMMATICAL LANGUAGE

Since the human mind automatically fills in missing elements or gaps in speech and visual images, you can use this idea to confuse, dis-orient, embed messages, etc. This work must be subtly done. Three examples follow:

> "Being is or was, soon, and now ... change."

> "Before you relax even more ... during ... while these thoughts ... helpful ... friendly ... aren't they not now ... but then ... for you..."

> "And, you do not know, no you do not, exactly how to change/ heal/learn/get what you want, but, ... when but?"

You can certainly have fun with these nongrammatical change statements. They are effective as Gilligan (1987, p. 244) states, "... non sequiturs will have maximum hypnotic effect when (1) they are delivered meaningfully (2) by a speaker assumed and expected to speak rationally and relevantly (3) in a context where the listener trusts the integrity of the speaker." The "shock" value of these statements means that they have to be used sparingly.

P. NEGATION

As you read this, close your eyes , and do *not* think about a pink polka-dotted tiger ... Human brains are wired such that you *first* have to create an image of the pink polka-dotted tiger *before* you can blank out that picture and, even then, the blanking out may not be perfect. Grinder and Bandler (1981, p. 67) state, *"No single pattern that I know of gets in the way of communication more often than using negation. Negation only exists in language and does not exist in experience."* [Emphasis in original.] There are several aspects to the use of negation, and they are discussed separately in what follows.

1. *Double Negatives and Tag Questions*—Double negatives generally require a pause for processing before it is understood that an affirmative is intended, and there are residuals of one of the negatives as the other is not heard. "Don't stop doing ..." "When you do not know what you really know, change can happen rapidly."

   Tag questions, at the end of a sentence, reinforce what came before, *even if* the tag statement is a negation.

   "And you can, can you not?"

   "And you will, won't you?"

   "And, you really do not know how fast you can change, do you?"

   Milton H. Erickson liked to establish rapport and minimize resistance in the first session by saying at an appropriate time, "Please be sure to *not* tell me anything that you do not wish to tell me." This is an elegant way to reassure a client, even though the embedded message is, "You can tell me anything— the choice is *yours*." This formulation should be kept in mind for single-session therapy.

2. *Apposition of Opposites*—This pattern consists of two opposing concepts or experiences that are juxtaposed within the same sentence or context. Partly, this is a confusion technique, yet the apposition also reinforces the tag concept or experience. Consider:

   "And you can remember to forget, can you not?"

   "I wonder if you really wish to remember to forget, or forget to remember."

   "As that toe itches a bit more, your comfort will increase."

   When opposites are in a single phrase that is an *oxymoron*. "How quickly can you slow down and escalate the decrease of that discomfort." "As you blindly look at yourself, what is it you are not seeing? "Just how smooth can your life be on that rocky road?"

3. *Not Knowing and Not Doing*—In this language pattern, the "not" is ignored, resistance is by-passed, and the client acts as if only positive statements were made. "You don't really have to do anything very different to change, do you?" "And, you don't have to listen to me since you already know what to do to take care of yourself, don't you?"

4. *Truisms and the "Yes Set"*—In using the "yes set" you make a series of statements and questions whose obvious answer is "yes," that is, they involve *truisms*. This establishes rapport, for you are affirming what the client already knows or experiences. "There really are many things that you know how to do for yourself." "You've already begun to think about ways to take care of yourself, haven't you?"

5. *Ambiguity*—The word "ambiguity" applies to the case where there is more than one deep structure to a surface structure—there is some doubt and uncertainty. Puns may be used for their ambiguity. There are several varieties of ambiguity.

   Phonological ambiguity occurs where words have the same sound sequences, but different meanings. These are homonyms such as: knows/nos/nose, dear/deer, way/weigh, weight/ wait, and to/too/two. The English language has many *individual* words which sound the same and have the same spelling, but have different meanings—it is the *context* that supplies the meaning. Some examples are: hold, ship, tire, cow, card, bowl, die, train, fast, and founder. Can you hold something *fast* to you while you are moving *fast*? Or, can you *train* a dog on a *train*?

   Syntactic ambiguity—occurs when the syntactic function of a word cannot be uniquely determined by the listener from the context in which the word is used. Some examples are:

   "... driving cattle can be dangerous."

"… investigating spies may be dangerous."

"… they are murdering crowds …"

Another form is the nominalization of a noun as in:

"The touching man …"

"The running bull …"

"The feeling of the bed …"

Punctuation ambiguity is a nongrammatical form where two unrelated sentences or ideas are connected by a word that can reasonably fit into both parts.

"Now you can notice your *hand* me that paper."
"And then you can take that *turn* around your life."
"When you're at the *store* away what you have learned."
"The clerk gave you the *change* that has already begun."

Q. BINDS

There are a variety of binds which have been well discussed by Erickson, Rossi and Rossi (1976, pp. 62–76) and by Erickson and Rossi (1979, pp. 42–9). The former book contains good definitions (pp. 6–64):

> A *bind* offers a free choice of two comparable alternatives—that is, whichever choice is made leads behavior in a desired direction. Therapeutic binds are tactful presentations of the possible alternate forms of constructive behavior that are available to the patient in a given situation. The patient is given free, voluntary choice between them; the patient usually feels bound, however to accept one alternative.

> Double binds, by contrast, offer possibilities of behavior that are outside the patient's usual range of conscious choice and control. … The double bind arises out of the possibility of communicating on more than one level. We can (1) say something and (2) simultaneously comment on what we are saying. … What is a bind or double bind for one person may not be for another.

Although the idea of binds and double binds may appear to be simple, their construction and delivery is not. Some examples follow:

"Would you like to deeply relax in this chair or that one?"

"Would you like to work on ways of changing your life now or in a few minutes?"

"Just how soon will your special healing begin its work?"

"Those old sensations of distress will safely and easily change to a mild and passing annoyance in how many minutes, or could it take as long as a day?"

"It doesn't really matter what your conscious mind does, because your inner mind will do just what it needs to in order to achieve that analgesia/anesthesia/relaxation/change you desire/healing."

A central characteristic of all binds is an *illusion of choice*. This is fostered frequently by mentioning *all* possible responses:

"Change may come about momentarily or in a few minutes, or at 10:16 pm this evening or, even, some time after that."

"This discomfort may increase temporarily for a moment, or it may stay the same, or it may have already significantly decreased."

4.2 Expectational Language—Suggestions, Implications and Presuppositions

Clients are highly suggestible in normal conversation, and are more so in a relaxed or hypnotic state. They expect to hear suggestions and comments and advice and interpretations, so their conscious and unconscious minds are open. This means that your words take on extra meaning, must be chosen carefully, and must be used with conscious intent. A word of caution. The unconscious mind tends to interpret words *literally* as in thinking of a "rest room" as a place to *rest*. This section specifically deals with those components of language that might be characterized as expectational, i.e., leading the client's thoughts, and are gathered under the headings of suggestions, implications, and presuppositions. In the author's practice, the primary expectation is that change can occur rapidly, effectively, efficiently and permanently.

A. SUGGESTIONS

Suggestions may be delivered directly or indirectly. Contrast the following two sentences:

"Close your eyes and relax."

"And, breathing softly and easily, becoming even more comfortable."

Ericksonians tend to use indirection more than direction, finding it effective and gentle and respectful. However, you always need to know your client and adapt your language appropriately.

Contingent suggestions imply a causal connection. "The more you pay attention to your breathing, the more relaxed you will become." That is, at some point the listener makes the connection between the two ideas, and then acts *as if* the second statement were true. This has the form of "when this ... then that".

Open-ended suggestions are those which emphasize choice and are deliberately vague. Open-ended suggestions are like master keys that can open many doors. Two examples are: "And, I don't know just when or whether your eyes will comfortably close, and you'll ..."; "Within your mind, now, you can safely drift off to your special healing/changing place."

B. IMPLICATIONS

The implication is generally made up of three parts: (1) a time-binding introduction of some kind; (2) the implied/assumed/intimated/ inted suggestion; and (3) some sort of *behavioral* response to signal when the implication has been accomplished. "I just don't know how, or how fast, you are going to change." "Just what is going to let you know that you have already changed, and are comfortable with those changes?"

C. PRESUPPOSITIONS

O'Hanlon (1987, p. 87) has defined a presupposition as "… the use of language, actions, and situations that *necessarily* involve certain antecedents *or* consequences." He also states, "Presupposition is a form of language in which certain ideas or experiences are presumed without ever being directly stated." The power of presuppositions is that they cannot be ignored and—if used correctly—create expectations for change that are outside or beyond the conscious mind. Examine the following examples for what is presupposed.

"Mary had a good day."

"I liked the way you did that."

"Change can be very helpful."

"Where is the heating pad?"

"Just how much change/healing/comfort/learning is possible?"

D. OVERLOADING

A speech pattern using lots of "ands" linking together many items has as its goal the *overloading* of the conscious and/or unconscious mind to ease into another state. "As you sit there *and* pay attention to your breathing *and* listen to the clock *and* feel the support of your chair *and* move a little when you need to *and* let your eyes de-focus *and* observe passing thoughts, how soon will you be deeply, deeply relaxed?" You just *stack* one set of realities/truisms on another until the mind just gives up and heeds the last suggestion.

E. LANGUAGE INVOLVING TIME

Consider the following sentence: "As you change, now, thinking about all of the new things you've already learned about yourself, then, and how, will you have already begun your healing process, even while you continue to progress even more, now?" Using time-related words and grammatical tense to confuse and presuppose that what you want *has already occurred* and all you need to do is discover and ratify it, *or* continue the already ongoing processes, is the power of this style. The use of time-related language takes practice.

4.3 Torpedo Style Language

A well-placed torpedo can sink a ship. In talk therapy, a well-phrased intervention can rapidly change a client. (The use of "torpedoes" was developed by NLP practitioners.) There are four components of a "torpedo": (1) use of temporal language; (2) use of reframes; (3) implications; and (4) congruence of delivery. Torpedoes are designed to be skeleton keys or *class-of-solution* interventions whose general nature covers many categories and encourages an internal transderivational search which is trance-like. Here are three examples taken from Battino and South (2005, p. 143):

> And as you sit there, now, your inner mind can wonder as to just how much you have changed, already, looking back on how you used to be, now, and thinking, soon, being, and what have you, will you, do differently?
>
> ...After this session is over, the work that you've started will have continued to be helping in what you have already done this afternoon, now, and you may be surprised, but, then again, not, now.
>
> ...And how surprised will you be, now, thinking over what has happened, then, when you soon, now, change to what you have been and had deserved?

Torpedoes obviously involve a level of confusion, and thus can reach the client on a deep unconscious level. They require practice in delivery since the pauses and marking out of words and phrases are crucial to their effectiveness.

4.4 Metaphoric Language

Chapter 2 in my book on the uses of metaphor (Battino, 2002, pp. 21–56) is on language usage for metaphoric work. In actuality, it is difficult to make meaningful distinctions between language for hypnotic work, metaphoric work, and very brief therapy. This means that there is much overlap between language usage in these three approaches. In this section, we will then just say a few words about things that are special to metaphor.

Basically, metaphors are stories, and stories are words strung together in grammatical patterns. If there is any specific language for metaphor, it is poetry since the power of a story is enhanced by the use of poetic language. Also, since poetry can be mesmerizing, one can consider speaking poetically to be akin to trance work. Snyder (1971) wrote a book whose title is *Hypnotic Poetry* (please note that this is a reprint of a book originally published in 1930). He placed poetry on a continuum from hypnotic to intellectualistic. With respect to commonalities in hypnotic poetry, Snyder (p. 37) found "… a peculiarly effective stimulus consists of words which fix the subject's attention by their rhythmic sound and make a simple suggestion on which the subject concentrates without any great mental activity." He also elucidated six characteristics which can be paraphrased as:

- An unusually perfect pattern of sound, which tends to be soothing.
- There is in these poems a freedom from abrupt changes (which can break the spell).
- The poems contain a certain vagueness of imagery.
- There are fatigue-producing elements which include verbal difficulties.
- The use of a refrain or frequent repetition.
- They tend to use suggestion on the entranced listener, the suggestions sometimes having a posthypnotic effect.

Good metaphoric language is most often surface structure, leading listeners to construct and create their own connections and meanings. Sometimes it is useful to be quite precise in terms of using deep structure language, and other times it is more useful to use vaguer language. If your work is client-centered (the "heroic" client), then you want to give the client every opportunity to develop their own solutions. You just have to be sensitive to your particular client's needs.

Chapter 13 in this book is specifically devoted to metaphoric approaches, and the subject will be dealt with in some detail at that point. Suffice it to say here that metaphors can be quite effective in very brief therapy.

4.5 Summing Up

Talk therapies use words, and it behooves the practitioner to be particularly skilled at using therapeutic language. This chapter has given a brief overview of language usage, emphasizing some of the important parts. In practice, you listen to your client and then respond—listening always comes first.

Perhaps the best illustration of how I use language would be to provide a transcript of a close-to-end-of-session brief hypnosis segment since this is common in my practice. That is, my clients know that I do hypnosis and expect that this will be a part of a session. I do not tape sessions so this is a reconstruction from my bare notes. Mary has been to see many doctors lately about pains in her legs that do not go away, and the medical tests have uncovered no cause for these pains. The pains make it hard for her to work and are, of course, painful. She was also worried that some of the possible undiagnosed causes mentioned as possibilities by the doctors might actually be true. Some of these were chronic diseases without any known treatments. Her safe haven was walking in the woods, and her healing imagery involved healing hands. Here is what I probably said:

Mary's Worries
Mary, I just like to start with paying attention to your breathing. You can notice each breath as it comes in and goes out, simply, easily, naturally. Just one breath at a time. And with each inhale your chest and belly softly rise. And, with each exhale, all of those

muscles relax. Simply, easily, naturally. This breath and the next one; this heart beat and the next one. Just one breath at a time. And, if I do not say just the right words or in the right way for you this afternoon, please feel free to change them so you get out of this experience exactly what you want, what you need at this time. Breathing softly and easily. This breath, and the next one. This is your healing time now, a special time, an interesting time, a time when you may learn some interesting things about yourself. Breathing comfortably, and finding that with each breath you relax even more. That's right, continuing to breathe easily. From time to time a stray thought may wander through your mind, notice it, thank it for being there, and go back to your breathing. This moment, this breath, your time now.

And, within your mind now you can just drift off to that special woods, that safe place, that place you like to walk through. Notice the path, and the trees, and the shrubs. Are there any roots crossing the path? Isn't the bark on that tree interesting? And, you may notice a slight breeze, so that as you look up you can see the tree tops swaying, and hear that soft sound of the leaves moving with the wind. Your time now. A healing time. As you walk along, you find a pleasant place to stop, to sit on a stone or a log, perhaps near some running water. Your woods, familiar and safe.

As you rest there, perhaps with your eyes closed, just listening to the woodsy sounds, and breathing in the special aromas, you become aware that something special, something interesting is going to happen. A pair of healing hands approaches—I don't know whose they are, but they are special to you and for you, and contain and know what it is you need to take care of you and to help with those pains in your legs. These hands are powerful and knowledgeable and know just what to do, and where to do it. Your healing hands. They come closer and make gentle contact with you, touching just the right places where their healing energy and knowledge and skills are needed. You can sense their presence, can you not? The gentle, yet powerful, healing touch, with the healing power moving through your skin and to all of those places in your legs and throughout your body where it is needed. Knowledgeable, skillful, powerful, effective. Re-arranging, re-adjusting, renovating, altering, fixing, making new connections here and severing poor and malfunctioning connections there, knowing just what to do and where to do this work. The healing hands are also working with your nervous system, changing, altering, adjusting, connecting and re-connecting, building and rebuilding, one nerve at a time, swiftly, easily, accurately, so that you are becoming more comfortable, more at ease. So what had been troubling you has already been corrected, and these are permanent healing changes. Your powerful healing hands continuing to work. And, these healing hands are also teaching your immune system, your body, your nervous system, your regulating systems, how to continue this healing work, moment by moment, minute by minute, day by day—just as long as you need this healing work to go on. Yes and yes and yes. Gently, easily, normally, naturally—your own body learning just what to do. And, when your healing hands have completed their work for now, they gently move away, having left behind so much for you. And, within your mind, you thank your healing hands for what they have done.

Mary, you know that your mind is somewhat like a tape recorder, so that whatever I have said, whatever has happened here this afternoon, is with you and available when you need it and as you need it. All you need to do is find a quiet place, pay attention to your breathing, drift off to your special safe woods, and replay what has been helpful to you. I want to thank you for your trust and your confidence. You have shown much courage in dealing with what has been troubling you, and in seeking out help in many places. You have much fortitude and inner strength.

When you are ready, you can just take a deep breath or two, stretch, blink your eyes, and come back to this room, here and now. Thank you.

The preceding is an example of a guided imagery healing session using hypnotic language and much of the material presented in this chapter. I deliberately did not put in emphases and pauses so that you, the reader, can play with just where and when and how they should be used. In the actual delivery of this material with Mary there were many pauses since she needed time to think and to process in her own way the ideas that were being mentioned. This session was an opportunity for Mary to learn, and to heal herself.

Chapter 5
Hypnosis and Very Brief Therapy

5.1 Rationale for Using Hypnosis

Since one of the things I do well is work with Ericksonian hypnosis and hypnotherapy, they somehow find their way into just about everything I do as a very brief therapist! The simplest rationale for my functioning this way is that that is what I do comfortably and naturally. In the previous chapter I trust that I have also provided some justification for using hypnotic language forms in this work since I find that the subtlety and indirectness involved appears to enhance effectiveness.

It is said that through hypnosis you can communicate directly with the client's unconscious or inner mind. If you function *as if* this were true, then you have a direct entrée to what many consider to be the controlling factor in a person's behavior, i.e., it is posited that the unconscious mind controls much of our conscious behavior. And, if we further assume (à la *The Heroic Client*) that it is the client who actually does all of the change work that we therapists take credit for, then this way of influencing the clients' ways of changing themselves is all to the good.

My working definition of hypnosis is "focused attention." In a session, I want the client's attention to be focused like tunnel vision on their singular task of finding useful ways to change their behavior. When a client is in a state of trance (however you define that—beyond focused attention), they are in a relaxed state and open to the suggestions that are part of a hypnosis session. In fact, the sense of *expectation* that meaningful change can and will occur in this session is heightened at a time when conscious control is relaxed. The client is more receptive to ideas of change, to surprising choices, to new possibilities, to variations of old activities and feelings, and to a future free of what had been troubling them. Their "resistance" is minimized and easily by-passed.

If you query a client at the end of a hypnosis session, they will tell you that they "consciously" heard everything you said, and that they also wandered off within their own mind following their own trains of thought from time to time. That is, they were actively listening, but some word, some suggestion, some idea, that you threw out kindled an internal search for related ideas and memories and possibilities. They will tell you that there were gaps in what they heard—returning from their own thoughts to listen again, and then wandering off again on their own. We presuppose that the unconscious mind actually heard and stored everything you said, but only certain parts of it are recalled at that time, the rest being available for future ruminations. The important work that occurs during a hypnosis session is by the client during those "gap" times when they are internally exploring their memories and the possibilities triggered by something you said. This is where, if you will, the "precise vagueness" of hypnotic language comes to the fore. Of course, one of the things that clients invariably comment upon is how *short* the hypnosis session was—time distortion is ever-present.

Although I consider hypnosis to be a mainstay of the way that I do very brief therapy, this kind of work can be done in many modalities that are not formally hypnosis—they may be "hypnotic," however! A particularly useful way to use hypnosis is to incorporate metaphor; this is discussed briefly in the next section, and at greater length in Chapter 13.

5.2 *Metaphor and Hypnosis*

In my model of doing effective therapy, I consider a principal task of the therapist is to provide a client with many choices. They are "stuck" and come to see you because they perceive that they have only one or limited choices in their lives. If you give suggestions of alternative behaviors directly, then you are into the strong possibility that you will end up playing the "Why don't you? Yes, but ..." game (of Transactional Analysis fame). Many well-protected clients are adept at deflecting alternatives that are presented directly to them. This means that you have to be subtle in providing alternatives. Within the framework of a hypnosis session, suggestions can be made directly, but it is better to make those suggestions using metaphors told to the client within the session. Of course, you can do metaphoric work without formal or informal inductions. Yet it is my conviction that any time you ask the client to do something where they "go inside", the client is in some level of trance, in so far as their attention is focused internally.

Metaphors are simply stories, and everyone loves to hear stories. Once you start telling a story and you get the client's attention, then while they are listening to the story you can insert a number of alternative ways for them to discover ways of changing. You just provide the framework in the plot and characters of the story—the client adds relevant detail that comes out of their own experience. In this sense, the client is doing the work by creating solutions based on their own unique life and experience. Although the story may contain many specific details, events and characters, the client picks up on the words, ideas and situations that make sense to them, and then adds relevant detail out of their own life experiences. Using a metaphor is like throwing out a bunch of bait and having a fish select the piece that is just right for it. The fish may snap at the nearest tidbit, or the juiciest looking, or be more finicky. Yet, snap they will, and once they are hooked, that bite initiates unique behavior. Specific information on this topic may be found in Chapter 13 as well as the author's book on the subject (Battino, 2002) and other sources cited therein.

Metaphors not only can be entrancing, they *are* entrancing. Hence, the connection between hypnosis and metaphor.

5.3 Hypnosis in Various Therapies

Without overly belaboring the point, it is my conviction that all therapies involve some level of trance. For example, within the Miracle Question approach discussed in the next chapter, the therapist elaborates on a miracle that occurs while the client is asleep. The gist of this miracle is that the client's concerns have been resolved. The therapist then spends time with the client going over in detail how their life will be different post-miracle. During this detailed elaboration of the client's post-miracle life the client has to go inside to think about all of the things that will have changed in their life. When you think about it, this internal focus guided by the therapist is a trance state. Thus, you can consider almost all therapeutic approaches to involve hypnotic states at some point. The EMDR procedure of repeated passes over the eyes is hypnotic. The carrying out of an ambiguous function assignment is similar to a post-hypnotic suggestion. As you read through the different ways of doing very brief therapy discussed in the following chapters, please consider how each one of them is related to hypnotic work. Before you accuse me of being single-minded about hypnosis, also understand that I believe it is possible to think about almost all forms of therapy as being variants of reframing or behavior modification!

Chapter 6
Solution-Oriented Approaches

6.1 The Work of de Shazer and Associates

The late Steve de Shazer and his wife Insoo Kim Berg of the Brief Family Therapy Center in Milwaukee have made some major contributions to psychotherapy. They are the primary promulgators of solution-oriented therapy, or solution-focused brief therapy (SFBT) as it is now called. Some useful references are: de Shazer (1985), de Shazer (1988), Miller and Berg (1995), Miller, Hubble and Duncan (1996), and Berg and Dolan (2001). The paradigmatic change that they proposed was to go from problem-oriented therapy to solution-oriented therapy. That is, rather than engage the client in talking about their problems—which they can do endlessly—the conversation is steered to solutions and what has been going well in the client's life. They found—and they are good systematic researchers—that if the therapist's orientation was to elicit "problem talk" by language and expectation, then the client would happily talk about problems, almost ad infinitum. After all, isn't that what you bring into the therapist's office, and what you talk about? The therapist is a presumed expert on problem-solving—they have all of those suggestions and know all of those techniques! On the other hand, they found that if you asked the client about what happened recently in their lives that they would like to continue and do more of, the client would respond with useful and good things that had happened in their lives. The Weiner-Davis et al. (1987) paper cited that clients would report about useful changes and experiences in their lives (if asked to do so) between the time of their calling in for an appointment and the appointment itself. They are not doing this to please the therapist, but are simply responding to a request for information. And this requested information was not about what was going wrong in their lives, but about what was going well! Seek solutions and ye shall find them …

I have heard de Shazer talk about one of the major outcomes of the solution-oriented approach for therapists. In effect, he asked if you as a therapist would rather spend your working days listening to all of the miseries that clients can pour out when discussing their problems, or would you rather listen to the shorter positive happy list of things that were going well? If you are a masochist, you would opt for problem talk.

And, once you have elicited examples of solutions in the client's life, you can then ask:

- What was different about that time?

- What can you do to maximize those positive outcomes so that they occur more frequently?

- Are there any other things in your life that are going well?

- How would you like your life to be different?

- How would you know when these useful changes have occurred?

- What would other people notice about you when these changes have occurred?

Even the most miserable client will find examples and exceptions to their troubles when asked to do so. "In the past week or two was there even a minute or two when you were feeling okay?" "Did your worries disappear or retreat to the background when you were brushing your teeth/showering/chewing/at the movies/making love/listening to music/reading a book/going to the toilet/buying groceries/cooking/sleeping?" Exceptions are there, but you have to ask for them.

When you consider solution versus problem orientations, you also have to consider the "as-if" phenomenon and behavior modification. That is, solution talk reinforces solution behavior; while with problem talk the client is re-living the miserable experiences they are talking about. If you ask a friend about his recent heart attack, and he starts giving you details about the experience, he will on some somatic and mental level be re-living that experience. As the client talks about how miserable she is she re-experiences that misery and can feel it intensely. Talking about depression can be depressing! Problem talk exacerbates the negative and eliminates the positive.

Berg has told about how she learned about the "miracle question" intervention from a client who wondered about what would happen in her life if a miracle occurred. In outline form the SFBT approach (paraphrased from Battino (2002, pp. 250–3) is:

1. Initially you ask: "What needs to happen that will let you know that today's session has been useful?" This focuses the session towards the client's choice.

2. "Since no trouble or concern happens all of the time, there must be exceptions, that is, times when things are pretty much okay. Please tell me about some of these exceptions."

3. The "miracle question" is then posed: "Suppose that tonight while you are asleep that a miracle occurs, and the miracle is that what prompted you to come to talk with me today is solved. This is a miracle. When you wake up tomorrow morning, what will have changed in your life? What will be different? How will you know that the miracle has occurred?" For the next fifteen to thirty minutes lead the client through as much detail as you can rally about how their life has been changed by the miracle. For example, "What would your spouse/children/parents/coworkers/boss/relatives/friends notice in your actions, behavior, and demeanor that would let them know that you have changed?" "If you were able to observe yourself somehow from outside, what would you notice that is different in the way you walk, stand, talk, behave after the miracle?"

4. At the next session find out how much of the miracle the client has experienced post-miracle. This validates the miracle question.

5. *Scaling questions*—These are generally on a scale of 1 to 10 and relate to: (1) a client's progress in treatment; (2) a client's level of hopefulness; (3) the amount of energy the client is putting into making life better; and (4) how much trust, confidence, willingness and motivation a client has. A typical scaling question would be: "On a scale of 1 to 10 where 1 stands for having no

confidence that you will overcome the difficulties you have been consulting me about, and 10 stands for complete confidence of a successful outcome, where are you today?" Fractions are permitted, such as 3.2, and small increments are encouraged as in "What would it take to move up to 3.7?" [The Miller/Duncan beginning and end of session questionnaires discussed earlier are an efficient form of scaling.]

6. "What will it take to make those successful things you have been doing occur again and continue?" Elicit details.

7. *End of session*—The therapist summarizes what has transpired, particularly with respect to solutions discussed, as in how the client overcame the odds against change. The client is complimented on what they have been doing. Homework along the lines of continuing what has been working is assigned.

Next session—Begins with asking about what has changed for the better since the last session.

This is, in a sense, a re-storying of the client's life with a future orientation and an emphasis via rehearsal of "as-if" changes. Remember that the detail on the changes are elicited by the therapist, but are *supplied* by the client. Therefore, the client is stating and creating the details about what has (and will) change. There are also three simple guiding principles of solution-oriented work. They are:

1. If it isn't broken, don't fix it.

2. If it has worked once, do it again.

3. If it doesn't work, then don't do it again—do something different.

There is a lot of common sense here.

I should note here that the miracle question or some variant of it is one of the most frequent things I do in my work. That is, it shows up in almost all of my sessions, one way or another. If the expectation is rapid change, why not have it occur as a miracle?

6.2 Miller and Duncan and Colleagues' Approaches

In the introductory material in Chapter 1, I got carried away by the importance of the work of Miller and Duncan and their colleagues and wrote extensively about what they have been doing and their recommendations and studies. Please consult that material as if it were at this point in the book! In particular, note how they use the Outcome Rating Scale at the beginning of each session to assess what has been going on in the client's life, and the Session Rating Scale for accurate feedback towards the end of the session. Without some way of obtaining feedback on what has been recently going on in the client's life and the client's perception of the current session, you are essentially working in the dark. The client is the expert on him or herself and needs to be consulted along the way. This is in contrast to imposing a diagnosis on the client and then mechanically applying whatever treatment protocols are called for in the EST (empirically supported treatments) materials. Recall that although the words "empirically supported" are used for these protocols, that they have been created for the theoretical client who conforms to a particular diagnosis and who is sufficiently obliging to respond to that treatment. Clients are unique and individual, while diagnoses are general and fuzzy and prone to error. Ask and ye shall be told.

6.3 Berg and Dolan and Miller's Wisdom

In Miller and Berg's book (1995, Chapter 3, pp. 32–65), they discuss six keys which are guidelines for using the miracle method. Although the book is specifically oriented to problem drinking, the wisdom contained therein is generally applicable. Their six "keys" follow with page citations for direct quotes:

> *Key 1:* Make sure your miracle is important to you. People are more likely to work hard to achieve a solution when it is one that is important to them. [P. 42.]

Key 2: Keep it small. ... the problem is usually not a lack of deter-mination but a failure to develop reasonable expectations of success. ... we always counsel our problem drinking clients to think small. [Pp. 44–5.]

Key 3: Make it specific, concrete, and behavioral. Actions taken by the client always need to be in specific, concrete, and behavioral terms. That is, what specifically will you notice in these and those situations on the day after the miracle occurs? What specifically will others notice? [P. 47.]

Key 4: Be sure you state what you *will* do rather than what you *won't* do. ... whenever you find yourself using words such as *no, never, don't, won't, can't, wouldn't,* or *shouldn't* to describe your miracle, substitute the words *yes, when, do, will, can, would,* and *should.* ... [an example is] "What shall I be doing instead of drinking?" [Pp. 52–4.]

Key 5: State how you will start your journey rather than how you will end it. With respect to post-miracle time, how will you know that the miracle has occurred? What will be the first sign that the miracle has happened? Who would be the first person to notice post-miracle changes in you? [P. 57.]

Key 6: Be clear about who, where, and when, but not why. ... There simply is no final answer to the question of why, since any answer that is given can be followed by another question of why. And we have observed that the most obvious result of such questioning is inaction. ... With regard to the who, our clients have found it helpful to consider the details of the desired change from the perspective of the important people in their lives. ... we encourage our clients to speculate on two different things once they have solved their problems: what their significant others will notice is different about them and what they will notice is different about their significant others. [Pp. 59–60.]

These six "keys" are a good guide to using the miracle question.

Berg and Dolan (2001) in their book of a collection of hope-inspiring stories involving the use of solution-focused-brief-therapy (SFBT), and emphasizing the use of the miracle method, wonderfully illus-trate their methods with many case histories and life stories. They make the miracle method come alive in a variety of contexts. The steps that they use have been outlined in Section 6.1 above. A few quotes from their book are relevant:

> ... the more we repeat the same story, the more realistic it seems. [P. xiv.]

> ... a distinguishing principle of the solution-focused approach is that the therapist empowers the client to retell their stories based upon their goals, rather than basing their goals upon their stories. [P. xiv.]

> In contrast to problem-solving, solution building as practiced in SFBT begins with the client's descriptions of how they want their lives to be different. It can be understood as beginning with the end of the story rather than the beginning of the problems. [P. 5.]

> The second step of solution building is to search for evidence or instances in which clients have experienced or are already experiencing bits and pieces of the desired life they identified in step one. [P. 5.]

6.4 Common Sense

To my mind, the solution-focused brief therapy approach is just plain common sense. By focusing on the problem (with its diagnosis) you are going down an almost endless road of exploring misery with your client. On the other hand, focusing on solutions is not only upbeat, it is effective, efficient and productive. The medical model is centered on problems that can be "fixed" by prescribed treatments. The "heroic client model", if you will, is centered on the client's capabilities, capacities, experience and knowledge, all of which the therapist assists the client in accessing. There is no magic pill administered by an all-knowing, all-powerful, therapist.

Instead, there is a collaborative undertaking to uncover and apply realistic solutions. I know which approach I prefer and, somehow in all of my sessions the emphasis is on solutions, and the miracle question sneaks in via some form or other.

Chapter 7
Bill O'Hanlon's Approaches

7.1 Inclusive Therapy

Bill O'Hanlon is an amazingly prolific and creative writer, and also an effective presenter. You can contact him at PossiBill@aol.com, and you should visit his website at www.brieftherapy.com for his latest activities, a free download of a current set of suggestions for therapists, a list of his books, and a list of where and when he is doing workshops. Some of his books that I have found particularly useful are (with their titles for reference): O'Hanlon and Wilk (1987) *Shifting Contexts: The Generation of Effective Psychotherapy*; O'Hanlon and Weiner-Davis (1989) *In Search of Solutions: A New Direction in Psychotherapy*; O'Hanlon and Martin (1992) *Solution-oriented Hypnosis: An Ericksonian Approach*; Cade and O'Hanlon (1993) *A Brief Guide to Brief Therapy*; O'Hanlon and Beadle (1997) *A Guide to Possibility Land: Fifty-one Methods for Doing Brief, Respectful Therapy*; O'Hanlon (2003) *A Guide to Inclusive Therapy: 26 Methods of Respectful Resistance-Dissolving Therapy*; and O'Hanlon and Rowan (2003) *Solution Oriented Therapy for Chronic and Severe Mental Illness*. In this section, we will be discussing inclusive therapy based on O'Hanlon (2003).

As with many useful and practical ideas, *inclusive therapy* is relatively simple and common-sensical. Clients and therapists alike tend to think *either/or* rather than *both/and*. Either a person is depressed or not, anxious or not, happy or sad, up or down, grieving or non-feeling, and a success or a failure, just to name a few dichotomies. Yet, can we not be oxymoronically happily sad or sadly happy, calmly tense or tensely calm, depressively active or actively depressed—all at the same time? O'Hanlon writes (O'Hanlon and Rowan, 2003, p. 15):

> I have found that for people suffering from complex dissociative and posttraumatic stress problems, as well as people diagnosed with borderline personality disorder, Inclusive Therapy is very

effective. Why? Because it recognizes the complex and contradic-
tory feelings they experience and the equally mixed messages
they communicate to others.

People are complex. Within the medical model you either have an
infection or cancer, for example, or you do not. Within the contextual real world model of actual people it is generally not either/or,
but both/and. If depression, for example, were a disease then there
would not be so many words and characteristics ascribed to it in the
DSM-IV. Rather, all depressed people would have the same symptoms to the same extent, or so many of them in common that there
would be consensus instead of discussion and debate. What
O'Hanlon's Inclusive Therapy does is take human variability into
account. His book contains 26 methods of working with Inclusive
Therapy. It is also short, pithy, contains many case histories, is
replete with illustrations, and provides the reader with exercises to
stretch their own mind for ways of implementing one of his methods. In this section I will highlight some of the 26 methods and their
rationale. You need to read and study his book to get a sense of the
usefulness of this material. Also, knowing how passionate I am
about reframing, please consider how much of the following can be
considered to be reframes.

O'Hanlon states that there are just three basic methods of Inclusive
Therapy. They are (p. 23):

1. Give the person permission to and permission not to have to
   experience or be something. For example, you can say, "You can
   feel angry and you don't have to feel angry."

2. Suggest the possibility of having seeming opposites or contra-
   dictions coexist without conflict. For example, you can say,
   "You can tell me and not tell me about the abuse." Or, "You can
   forgive and not forgive at the same time."

3. Allow for the opposite possibility when speaking about the
   way it was, is, or will be. You can say, "That was either a terrible
   thing or it wasn't."

I trust you are beginning to understand the usefulness and power of
inclusivity.

Under the heading of "The Permissive Method", O'Hanlon gives 12 methods. He also provides "theory breaks" at various junctures to help you understand the "why" of particular methods. A few of the 12 methods are highlighted here using O'Hanlon's notation:

1.1 Give permission for any and all experiences, feelings, thoughts, and fantasies the person may have. ... The point here is that some people need permission to feel what they feel. ...it is just as important for some people to receive permission not to feel what they don't feel. [Pp. 26–7.]

1.2 Give permission not to have to experience, fantasize, think, feel, or do something. ... You don't have to act on your feelings or fantasies. It's okay to have them, though. It doesn't necessarily mean anything bad about you to have them. [Pp. 30–1]

1.3 Give permission to and not to have to. ... You can feel angry and you don't have to feel angry. [P. 35.]

1.4 Speak about the concern so as to convey it is in the realm of normal human experience, rather than an exotic or terrible thing. [P. 38.] [I recently had a client who needed to hear that his responses to the unusual conjunction of a whole bunch of cata-strophic things in his life were "normal" and not that he was so depressed that a doctor had to prescribe anti-depressants. That is, anyone would be somewhat depressed if they had to go through what he was going through.]

Theory Break on the importance of "and" [P. 48.]—[Consider how the sentence] "I want to stay in bed, but I have to go to work" [changes when turned into] "I want to stay in bed and I have to go to work".

1.8 Include the other side of the equation in a phrase consisting of opposites (oxymoron) or in separate parts of the same phrase or sentence. ... Client: I am anxious about the upcoming exam. Therapist: You can calmly observe that anxiety to notice whether it helps you or not. [Pp. 49–51.]

1.10 Accept and allow the resistance or the problem, but contain it in space, time or mode of expression. ... You seem to be having a great deal of difficulty going into trance in that chair, I suggest you move to the other chair, and we'll continue. [P. 54.]

1.12 Employ paradoxical striving. Encourage people to make their symptom or problem worse. [P. 65.] [Please note that this is related to Frankl's "paradoxical intention." O'Hanlon adds a caution about not encouraging harmful, illegal or destructive acts.]

In the section on validation and change, O'Hanlon describes five methods, three of which are listed here:

2.1 Acknowledge with the past tense. Let people know you have heard or accepted their feelings, problems, or points of view, while locating them in the past. [P. 73.]

2.2 Acknowledge with partial instead of global reflections. Change people's statements from global, all-or-nothing statements into more modulated, partial statements through reflection. ... I usually introduce only small modifications, going from all-or-nothing to *usually, mostly, often, most of the time, almost always, typically*, and so on. [Pp. 76–7.]

2.5 Acknowledge while adding expectancy or possibilities for change. Reflecting while adding words or phrases that give a sense that change is possible or expected in the future. [P. 91.]

In the section on spirituality and the inclusive self there are 7 methods. Briefly, they are (3.1 to 3.7, pp. 95–119): connect to the body; connect to the deeper self, the soul or the spirit; connect to another being; connect to a group or community; connect to nature; connect through art; connect to God, the universe, a Higher Power or some other transcendent being. Finally, in a section on bigotry, there are two methods:

4.1 Elicit self-compassion. Find a way to help people soften and become more accepting, less judgmental toward themselves. [P. 126.]

4.2 Elicit compassion for others. Find a way to help people soften and become more accepting and less judgmental of others. ... Compassion is not forgiveness. Nor does it involve excusing other people's harmful or bad behavior. [Pp. 128–9.]

And a few gems:

Don't marry your hypotheses. [P. 134.]

Be inclusive, except when you aren't. Be flexible, except when that doesn't work. [P. 139.]

Inclusive Therapy is deceptively simple, yet it works.

7.2 Brief, Respectful Therapy

O'Hanlon believes in possibility for his clients, and he wrote a book with Beadle (O'Hanlon and Beadle, 1997) that is a "guide to possibility land", that contains 51 methods for doing brief, respectful therapy. Again, I will only cite several of these methods, and urge you to read and study the book.

1. Carl Rogers with a twist—Like Carl Rogers, we accept people where they are right now, and help them accept themselves. But then we add a little twist. We communicate, "where you are now is a valid place to be, AND you can change." … Possibility language involves a number of different ways of using language to break up and rearrange what the client knows in order to facilitate change. How we speak about ourselves and our lives can influence feelings in subtle and profound ways. Small changes in our repeating mental talk can make a big cumulative difference in how we feel and, even, to a certain extent, how we act. [P. 15.]

2. Possibility-laced acknowledgment—Let clients know that you have heard and understood their suffering, their concerns, their felt-experience and their points of view, without closing down the possibilities for change. [P. 17.]

3. Validate and value clients' being and inner experience, while holding them accountable for their actions. [P. 25.]

4. Give permission for being—Let the client know it is OK to have automatic experiences such as sensations, involuntary thoughts, feelings, and images. [P. 26.]

5. Use humor or anything that gets the clients to see their situation as less grim, without disrespecting or minimizing their pain and suffering. [P. 32.]

6. Assume past and present problem-free times. Ask and talk about problem-free times, even if they only occurred while the person was unconscious! [P. 33.]

7. Assume the client is an active agent in his or her life—suggest that any success was a result of the client's efforts. [P. 34.]

8. Depathologize by changing labels—change devaluing or pathological labels to more everyday, nicer, more change-available ways of talking about difficulties. [P. 37.]

9. Depathologize by framing the difficulty as a stage—speak about the problem or concern as a developmental stage, something that the person might grow out of or get over. [P. 38.]

10. Normalize—speak about the concern as if it were in the realm of normal human experience, rather than an exotic or terrible thing. [P. 40.]

11. Externalize the problem—put the problem outside the client by personifying it, or seeing it as a set of behaviors, so it can be grappled with more easily. [P. 42.] [Externalization is a method used in Narrative Therapy. See White and Epston (1990) and Chapter 16.]

12. Specify goals—negotiate achievable goals in videotalk, in terms of actions or results that could be seen on a videotape. [P. 48.]

13. Presuppose that the goal will be achieved—Assume that therapy will be successful. Use words like "will," "when," and "yet," when speaking about clients' therapy goals and post-therapy goals. ... Remember that language is a virus, and it is likely if you presuppose success, your clients will be infected with your confidence regarding their goal achievement. [P. 55.] [This is a wonderful statement of the thesis of this book!]

14. Evoke an experience of resourcefulness—Use examples from the client's own history to evoke the inner experience of resourcefulness. [P. 61.]

15. Times without the problem—Examine in detail how the client felt and acted when the current difficulty did not occur, even just for a moment. [P. 63.]

16. Find what worked—Get detailed descriptions of what has worked for the client in similar situations, or talk about what worked for other people in this difficulty. [P. 65.]

17. How come it didn't get worse?—Ask clients to explain to you what has restrained them from going further in their problem patterns. [P. 69.] [This is a variant of 16.]

18. Find the ending or stopping pattern—Ask clients how they stopped the problem or what they started doing once it was going or went away. [P. 70.]

19. Compare and contrast—Compare times when the difficulty occurs with when it does not occur, emphasizing actions under the client's control. ... [the client says, "My depression is what I want to work on." and the therapist responds] "So tell me about a typical day when you were depressed, the first thing you do in the morning, then compare that with a day when you are feeling better and less depressed." [P. 74.]

20. Design pattern interventions—Intervene in several of the small ways details of the way a problem pattern is played out, until you discover one that changes or eliminates the pattern. [O'Hanlon gives a list of 14 ways to change the pattern such as changing the frequency, time, location and duration of the pattern.] [P. 75.]

21. Anticipate and plan relapse prevention—Things don't always go smoothly in the course of making significant changes, and it's OK to let the client know this. Just make it clear that it is temporary, that the change part is what counts, and that things will soon get back on track. [P. 79.] [Predicting a relapse removes its power.]

In the preceding, I have outlined just 21 of the 51 methods that O'Hanlon and Beadle present in detail with examples. Their book obviously needs to be studied, and you need to keep all of these methods in mind (if you can!). Remember that in any complex interaction, the component with the most variability controls. With respect to doing therapy, the more variability you have, and the more flexibility, then the more effective you will be.

7.3 Hypnosis in O'Hanlon's Work

From the time of his training with Milton H. Erickson, O'Hanlon has incorporated hypnosis into his practice. At the present time he continues to do training in Ericksonian hypnosis and hypno-therapy—check his web site (cited above) for times and locations. In his early book on Ericksonian methods (1987) he goes over in detail the underlying principles of this work. This is an useful book to read on the subject and, in his style, is brief and to the point.

O'Hanlon's book with Rowan (2003) is specifically on doing solution-oriented therapy for clients who have chronic and severe mental illness. There are, again, many useful methods discussed for what many continue to believe is a special and particularly difficult population with which to work. Hypnosis is part of this work, too, and the authors cite Jay Haley (1963) as noting (p. 61),

> ... the similarities between psychotic and hypnotic experiences. Both can involve distortions of perceptions, depersonalization, hallucinations, and automaticity of behavior and experience. The crucial difference is that, in hypnosis, people feel OK about themselves and their experiences. In psychosis, people feel badly about themselves and their experiences. ... Our approach, then, is to revalue people and their experiences.

O'Hanlon is a major contributor to useful and interesting ways of working with clients. I particularly like the way he is open to changing his methods and following their evolution. His work is worth following.

Chapter 8
Lucas Derks's Social Panorama

8.1 Introduction

Given my fixation on reframing, it is always exciting to come across a new and different way to reframe (even if the author may not think of his contribution in these terms). Nevertheless, I am allowed my prejudice of thinking of Lucas Derks's new book (2005) as a major contribution to the literature on reframing, and a fascinating way of working with clients. One might even consider it to be a paradigmatic shift as in Kopp's changing from therapist-centered to client-centered metaphors.

Derks states in his postscript with respect to "social panoramas" that this is, "The first book on the subject ever to see the light of day." As such, Derks has made an important contribution in providing a well-researched primer on the subject. Although this may be considered to be an elaboration of the NLP "Swish" technique (or changing personal history, or time line therapy), and an extension of E. T. Hall's "proxemics" (Hall, 1959), it is much more. The social panorama is a major breakthrough in how to think through and work through a client's "stuckness". To Derks, a client is stuck *spatially*—two- and three-dimensionally—in a particular social panorama. His brilliant solution is to have the client alter and adjust their social panorama (and their position in it) so that they are no longer bound or controlled by the old configuration. In that sense, you might even consider this to be a kind of spatial reframing that is connected to Satir's family sculpting or Moreno's psychodrama, but in a more streamlined and effective format. Derks has in fact created almost endless "techniques" (61 of them!) for working through various concerns. After an abbreviated discussion about the theory of his approach, I will detail a few of those techniques in the next section. His chapter on the spiritual panorama is especially interesting for its insights on the subject. The chapter on training is quite pragmatic. This new work by Derks is a fascinating and practical way to help clients "see" themselves in new and useful life panoramas. That kind of seeing sets them free! I recommend this book highly; it is well-worth studying in detail.

Derks considers "personification", which is the mental representation of somebody to be central to his approach. He differentiates five types of personifications (p. 8):

> *Self-personification*—the representation of the self.
>
> *Other-personification*—the representation of other individuals.
>
> *Group-personification*—the representations of groups and large social complexes …
>
> *Spiritual personification*—the representation of dead and non-human social entities such as ghosts, spirits, and gods.
>
> *Metaphorical personification*—physical objects, abstractions, animals, plants, symbols, processes and non-human-non-spiritual entities to which are ascribed human-like qualities.

About these, he says (p. 9):

> We invent all these different types of personification. We create an image, put it in a particular place, attribute feelings, drives and a wealth of other features to it, and then save the whole thing in our memory. After that we start to behave as if the thing in our mind is a real flesh and blood person. From that moment on we believe that this person really exists in the way that we have created them.

Derks then lists nine self-personification factors (p. 13):

> *Location*—my awareness that I am here and others are there.
>
> *Abilities*—my awareness that I can do things, such as moving, talking, reasoning.
>
> *Drives and motivation*—my awareness that I want something.
>
> *Feelings*—my awareness of emotions, bodily sensations and pain.

Self-awareness—my knowledge of who I am among others.

Perspective—my awareness that I see things my way; my beliefs.

Spiritual connection—my awareness of my connection with the whole.

Perceivability—my awareness that I can be seen, heard and felt.

Name—I know what I am called.

These are ways of knowing who we are. A defining idea in cognition is that (p. 16), "Everything that exists has its own place in the universe and anything without a place does not exist at all." That is, we think and process information *spatially*.

About his approach, Derks states (p. 26):

> The social panorama model is a tool for analysing and solving problems in social life. The model has the images of people, called personifications, as its elements. Change in a personification will be brought about on the level of its components, the 'personification factors.' Location is defined as the primary personification factor; a change in location will necessarily change the relationship involved. Quite often the therapist needs to change one of the other personification factors first in order to make a personification move in someone's social panorama.

Indeed, Derks considers that the primary diagnostic tool in social panorama-based therapy to be finding the *locations* of the problematic personifications. In his Technique 4, which is a demonstration to groups or individuals about how they create their place in the social world, he has them imagine that they are experiencing themselves as part of all mankind, and to feel that they are surrounded by all other people in the world. Then, they are to observe their reactions to: (1) having all the people of the world come closer to them; (2) move upwards; (3) move further away; (4) move below them; and (5) turn and look away from you. These are all submodality (see Chapter 15) changes. The ones Derks mentions are: intensity and absence, hard-to-find-personifications, bi-location (person in two places), association/dissociation (being in the image or observing it), front/back, up front (as in 12 noon), vertical (above eye level), horizontal (left/right), darkness/light, temperature (often overlooked), movement, orientation, and clustering of personifications. They all involve changing perspectives. A basic assumption is (p. 67), "… 'relationship equals location'. The problematic personification is in the wrong location; a better feeling will result from moving it to another site."

Throughout his book, Derks lists a number of assumptions. Number three is (p. 74), "Personifications cannot be deleted but can only be transformed by changing personification factors (mainly location, abilities and perspective)." He then lists two major methods of intervention (p. 74):

a. Moving personifications to better locations by means of direct suggestion (e.g., draw it closer, make it lower, and push it sideways).

b. Improving personifications by means of widening their abilities or changing their beliefs. (Most often this is done by 'transferring resources.')

8.2 Some Examples of Social Panoramas

With respect to working with families, Derks identifies three levels of social cognitive systems within a family. They are systems of interconnected social representations that influence each other. These three levels are (pp. 205–6):

Personifications: System level 1. A personification constitutes a system with the personification factors as its elements (parts). A change in one factor will affect the other personification factors. …

Social panoramas: System level 2. This system has the personified family members as its elements, as these function subjectively within the mind of the individual client. …

Social reality: System 3. This consists of the system of real family members. These members all carry family panoramas in their minds and interact with one another and think about one another on the basis of these images.

Obviously, what happens in the client's family panoramas affects the lives of the other real family members. Also, the communication between them is affected by the way that family members see, hear, and feel their relatives in their minds.

Derks goes on to say (pp. 206–7):

> Families usually expend a lot of energy convincing one another of how they "should" see one another. This social "norming" usually uses all four channels of relational communication:
>
> 1. Naming relationships. (He is my brother)
>
> 2. Speaking of locations. (You are above your sister)
>
> 3. Showing locations. (Gestures and pointing to locations)
>
> 4. The use of metaphors. (We come from a warm nest)

Since everyone grows up in a different environment and contexts, it is not surprising that children from the same family can grow up with very different family panoramas.

To give you a flavor of how Derks works, we now cite his Techniques 42, 43, 44 and 45 (pp. 247–50). This starts at the point where an objective that involves a deep-rooted social behavior pattern has been formulated and an early childhood family panorama has been mapped.

Technique 42: Transference of abilities to the distant family past

1. In your family, whose lack of abilities stimulated the development of the limiting social behavior?

2. Once that family member has been found, the missing abilities are given names (X, Y, Z ...).

3. Call up these abilities one at a time. Choose a specific moment when you had the ability very strongly. Get right into the situation. Associate each ability with its own color and prepare it for a metaphorical transfer with a time machine.

4. Go back (with the time machine) into the past, taking the abilities with you (X, Y, Z …). Find the family member who needs them when he or she was a young child (e.g. Go back to the time when your father was six years old, taking with you the abilities he lacked).

5. Make good contact with the young family member and transfer the abilities to him or her, one at a time, by using their color.

6. Visualise how the family member grows up enriched by the abilities (X, Y., Z …). Take your time, follow that line to just before the moment your parents first met.

7. Visualise the contact between your parents with the abilities present. Continue until your conception.

8. Experience how the abilities (X, Y, Z …) affect your older siblings. Take your time to feel the abilities (X, Y, Z …) being present all around you when you are in the womb, and then experience an easy birth.

9. Experience how you are received and grow up in a family in which the abilities (X, Y, Z …) affect everyone. Grow up until you reach the age at which you have explored the family panorama (e.g., five years old).

10. Check how the abilities (X, Y, Z …) have helped to change the family panorama.

To prevent inconsistencies in the family panorama, follow Technique 43.

Technique 43: Testing locations in the second perceptual position

1. Move, in your mind, to the location of a random family member (second perceptual position). How does that family member like the new situation? What does it feel like to be there? How do the others appear from that spot?

2. Notice any objections that arise.

3. Make small adjustments until you know exactly where the objections are.

4. Move on to the next personification and do the same thing. Experiment with small changes in location and direction of gaze until this one, too, is satisfied.

5. Go on until all personifications, including yourself, are satisfied.

Technique 44 is used "to promote the transfer from the therapeutic context into real life". Once the new family panorama has been approved by all the family personifications, proceed with:

Technique 44: Stabilising the family panorama

1. Let the client assimilate the new image.

2. Move around in and possibly outside the space in which you have been working. While you move, have the client imagine different contexts: holiday, work, shopping, visiting, alone in the woods. Let the client imagine the new image in those contexts.

3. Repeat this for as long as necessary to be sure that the client will remember it always and everywhere.

And, lastly, in this series, the following technique is used to integrate the new image in life history.

Technique 45: Growing up into the present

Now ask the client to grow up from their new (five years of age) family panorama into the present. Give the client as much time as they need, and encourage them to imagine all the changes which might have happened as realistically as possible, complete with feelings. This reliving has a particularly stabilising influence. If necessary, if the client's attention has been taken by regret about missed chances, help them to get back to a future-oriented attitude.

The process involves imagination and going in and out of the imagined space, adjusting and altering place and attitude to maximize the client's sense of who they are in their own social panorama. As you may notice, it is heavily NLP based.

In Chapter 7 on the spiritual panorama, Derks comments that it was just as easy to find the locations of dead people, ghosts and gods as it was for the personifications of living people. He also found that people usually represent their spiritual personifications far away, that is, from six to one hundred mental meters distant. It turns out that personifications are extremely difficult to erase. However, they can be transformed and moved and improved with added abilities. Success is more likely when you look for the positive intentions of the possessing evil spirit (as in Bandler and Grinder's six-step reframing procedure). Adding abilities which these evil spirits lack is just as effective with them as it is with hated parents or dreadful colleagues.

I conclude this section with a technique for dealing with grief, and another for reconciliation with ancestral spirits (a minimal description of six-step reframing) (pp. 316–17).

Technique 47: Dealing with grief

1. In the social panorama, find the location of the dead person who is giving problems.

2. Find the peaceful locations of other dead people with whom there are no problematical feelings of grief.

3. Move the troublesome dead person to the peaceful location.

Technique 48: Reconciliation with ancestral spirits

1. Help the client to determine what the positive intention of the ancestral spirit is.

2. Together with the client, search for alternative behavior that could help achieve the positive intention of the spirit.

3. Suggest these alternatives to the spirit and ask for a clear signal if he agrees.

8.3 Summing Up

The social panorama approach involves having the client search the imaginary landscape in which they populate their existence to notice what is there, and how these entities relate to each other. The dysfunctions in their life and the stuck places become evident in their social panorama. Using the variations available using sub-modalities in terms of changing location, shape, color, distance etc., they can modify their panorama for their own benefit. This is a way of changing their perception of their life in the social contexts in which they actually live. And once those perceptions change, and once they have altered and modified the relationships in it in this interesting intervention, then they are actually into a new set of life patterns.

This chapter is but a brief introduction to the possibilities of working with social panoramas. Derks's book, with its case studies and examples and theoretical background and many techniques, needs to be studied carefully. For me, it was an exciting new way to think about working with clients.

Chapter 9
Erickson and Very Brief Therapy

9.1 Utilization Principle

The work of Milton H. Erickson was quite hard to characterize—he just refused to be pigeon-holed. A recent valuable attempt has been made by Short et al. in *Hope & Resiliency: Understanding the Psychotherapeutic Strategies of Milton H. Erickson, MD*, which defines several key components that made him successful as a therapist (Short, Erickson and Erickson Klein, 2005). It has been said of him (although this is, of course, an exaggeration) that he created a new therapy for every client. If you study his writings and cases, there are a number of common themes and methods. He liked to use metaphor and was a famous story-teller. Most students of Erickson's work find two things that exemplify his approach. The first is in how he did hypnotic work. He broke with the tradition of his time by using indirect approaches rather than the authoritarian direct approach that was standard. In the early days of hypnosis they talked about the hypnotist being the "operator" and the client being the "subject". The hypnotist was in charge and controlled the responses and behavior of the client. With Erickson's use of what has been described as the precise use of vague language, the client filled in the details and did the work. Erickson was thus indirect and permissive in the way that he did hypnosis. Yet, if you read his case histories, you will find that he was also a master of the direct approach, and could be quite forceful and directive. As an effective therapist you have to be able to be both directive and indirect, forceful and subtle, adapting your approach to the client and their needs. (Please note that this is an example of "inclusivity" on the part of the therapist!)

The second thing that Erickson developed and promulgated and used was the *utilization approach*. Erickson considered every client, indeed every human being, to be absolutely unique and individual. If the client is unique, then what you do to help them must also be unique. Of course, it is always possible to make generalizations about the behavior of people such that we can describe classes of responses and reactions. In practice, this means that we need to be sufficiently flexible to devise and employ variants of methods we are skilled at using. In Chapter 7, a seemingly endless number of O'Hanlon's methods were briefly described. Which one do you use with a particular client, and when? The simple answer is to use the method or methods that fit that particular client's concerns and difficulties during that session. There is always a "negotiation" at some level over what to do and, if you believe in "the heroic client" being preeminent, then it is the client who controls what is done. The method needs to be matched to the client, and not vice versa.

Erickson was a student of mythology and anthropology and liked to tell the story of the Greek thief Procrustes who was in the habit of kidnapping people. Let me quote from my unabridged dictionary about Procrustes, "A celebrated legendary highwayman of Attica, who tied his victims to an iron bed, and, as the case required, either stretched or cut off their legs to adapt them to its length. Hence, the *bed of Procrustes* or *Procrustean bed*, an idea, theory, or system to which facts, human nature, or the like, would be arbitrarily fitted." If you are a true believer in some given approach and apply that to all of your clients, you are in danger of becoming another Procrustes. Bill O'Hanlon quotes a colleague as saying, "Whenever I get a hypothesis about what is going on with a client, I lie down until it goes away." Which is more important: proving your theory of change and how you implement it, or finding ways to help this particular client?

In applying the utilization approach, you simply observe and utilize the client's observable and nonobservable behaviors and beliefs. The "nonobservables" are what the client says about him or herself. When these behaviors are paced you establish rapport, and then "leading" helps move the client along. Mainly, you listen to discover what is unique about this particular client. Then you work within the client's belief systems and history and capabilities. If your client is a devout Catholic (or devout believer in any system), then you use that knowledge in working with them. If your client is a woodworker or a knitter or a physician or a pharmacist or a day laborer or a housewife/mother or a checkout clerk, then you "utilize" who they are and what they do in your approaches to helping them find ways to help themselves, and within the framework of what they know. This does *not* mean that it is improper to help them find ways of extending their horizons and capabilities and activities—who and what they are now is used in a kind of judo to enhance and extend themselves. That is, start with what they are familiar with rather than drop them cold turkey into the deep end of the swimming pool to find out if they can learn to swim! (Within the field of education this is called "constructionism" since you *construct* new ideas and learning on what it is the student already knows.) On the other hand, if your belief system or singular method of doing therapy is going to get in the way of helping this unique client, then you need to refer the client to someone else. I know of a devout atheist who comfortably works with most devout Christians, yet I have known him to refer clients.

Listen, utilize, and beware of Procrustes!

9.2 Practicality

Erickson was a pragmatist who was always more concerned with ways to help clients change than with theory. Early on, he dropped psychoanalysis, and he made these relevant comments about working with patients (Zeig, 1980, pp. 268–9):

> I think that you should take a patient as he is. He is only going to live today, tomorrow, next week, next month, next year. His living conditions are those of today.

> Insight into the past may be somewhat educational. But insight into the past isn't going to change the past. If you were jealous of your mother, it is always going to be a fact that you *were* jealous of her. If you were unduly fixated on your mother, it is always going to be the fact. You may have insight, but it doesn't change the fact. Your patient has to live in accord with things of today. So you orient your therapy to the patient living today and tomorrow, and hopefully next week and next year.

He viewed insight as something that the client would discover on their own as needed, and that it was not the task of the therapist to supply—it was frequently a useful byproduct, but not the goal. The previous citation is that of an eminent pragmatist.

Clients visit therapists expecting the therapist to help them get out of a behavior or attitude within which they are stuck. Although it almost seems to be human nature to avoid change and stick with the usual, when the usual is disturbing and uncomfortable and interferes with daily living, then change is the answer. (The psychiatrist Carl Hammerschlag states that change is the human condition, and that the only people who are not changing are dead.) Being aware that all journeys must start with a single step, Erickson worked to have the client change in some small way, almost an infinitesimal way. The "theory" and the practice is that once a particular behavior or attitude is broached, then the client becomes aware that change is possible. One of Erickson's clients had a phobia for driving beyond the city limits. Erickson got the client to put on his best suit of clothes, drive to the city limits, and then drive one telephone pole beyond those limits and park off the side of the road. At that point the client was to get out of his car, walk over to the roadside ditch, and roll in it in his new suit. Then he was to get back in his car and drive to the next pole, and repeat the process. This is both an example of an ordeal (see Chapter 10) and "salami" tactics, that is one slice at a time. Obviously, Erickson convinced this desperate client that it was possible for him to survive driving the distance of just one telephone pole. The client lost his phobia.

If you can get a client to "violate" their phobia in some very small way, then you have established that confronting the phobia is both possible and volitional and under their control. Recall that one of the tasks of a therapist is to change behavior that the client knows is involuntary and beyond their control, to voluntary and within their control. One of O'Hanlon's methods is normalizing behavior, and this apparently small reframe opens the way to change.

Being pragmatically practical, and one small step at a time ...

9.3 Stories and Metaphors

Erickson[2] was a master story-teller, and had a fund of stories that he adapted to each client and circumstance, as well as using them in his teaching seminars. The use of metaphors was one of his favorite ways of teaching, particularly later in his life. Zeig (1980, pp. 7–18) has given eight reasons for the value of anecdotes (or metaphors) in therapy. They are:

- anecdotes are nonthreatening

- anecdotes are engaging

- anecdotes foster independence—the person needs to make sense of the message and then come to a self-initiated conclusion or a self-initiated action

- anecdotes can be used to bypass natural resistance to change

- anecdotes can be used to control the relationship

- anecdotes model flexibility

- anecdotes can create confusion and promote hypnotic responsiveness

- anecdotes tag the memory—"They make the presented idea more memorable."

Anecdotes are also respectful and gentle. For more detailed information on the uses of metaphor in psychotherapy and in Erickson's work, consult the references in the footnote below, and the references within them.

_____

[2] With respect to Erickson's use of metaphors, see Battino and South (2005) Chapter 11 (pp. 307–36) on basic metaphors; Chapter 12 (pp. 337–54) on advanced metaphors; Chapter 13 (pp. 355–62) on metaphor therapy and guided metaphor; and Chapter 14 (pp. 363–78) on the arts as hypnotherapeutic metaphors. Also, see Battino (2002) for his book on the uses of metaphor. Finally, see Chapter 13 in this book for metaphoric approaches.

In this section, we will just reproduce three of Erickson's teaching tales from Rosen (1982).

Being Six Years Old [p. 162]

I received a letter from my daughter-in-law last week in which she told me about her daughter's sixth birthday. The next day she did something for which her mother reprimanded her, and she told her mother: "It's awfully hard to be six years old. I've only had one day's experience."

He Will Talk [pp. 58–9]

A lot of people were worried because I was four years old and didn't talk, and I had a sister two years younger than me who talked, and she is still talking but she hasn't said anything. And many people got distressed because I was a four-year-old boy who couldn't talk.

My mother said, comfortably, "When the time arrives, then he will talk."

Scratching Hogs [p. 59]

One summer I sold books to pay my way through college. I walked into a farmyard about five o'clock, interviewed the farmer about buying books, and he said, "Young fellow, I don't read anything. I don't need to read anything. I'm just interested in my hogs."

"While you're busy feeding the hogs, do you mind if I stand and talk to you?" I asked.

He said, "No, talk away, young fellow, it won't do you a bit of good. I'm not going to pay attention to you; I am busy feeding the hogs."

And so I talked about my books. Being a farm boy, I thoughtlessly picked up a pair of shingles lying on the ground and started scratching the hogs' backs as I was talking. The farmer looked over, stopped, and said, "Anybody knows how to scratch a hog's back, the way hogs like it, is somebody I want to know. How about having supper with me tonight and you can sleep overnight with no charge and I will buy your books. *You like hogs.* You know how to scratch 'em the way they liked to be scratched."

9.4 Tasks and Ordeals

Erickson liked to use tasks and ordeals to get clients to change. (Ordeals are discussed in the next chapter, and a variation on them called "ambiguous function assignments" are discussed in Chapter 11.) An example of an ordeal was cited above with the young man who put on a new suit and drove to the edge of town. Erickson's particular skill was in motivating clients to actually carry out these tasks. He implied or stated directly that doing what might be considered in normal circumstances to be something silly or unusual contained within it the solution to their concerns. Erickson's expectation was that the client would discover solutions in the carrying out of the task—so it turned out to be! With respect to tasks and ordeals, in particular, the basic idea is that if you make it more difficult for a client to have a symptom than to give it up, then the client gives up the symptom. And despite what psychodynamic traditions say, giving up a symptom generally leads to permanent change (rather than symptom substitution). This is one of the things that Erickson discovered that led him away from Freudian approaches.

Tasks can be described as being homework that the client agrees to do. These may be trying out different behaviors in the as-if mode, paradoxical injunctions like prescribing the symptom, reading particular materials, and the various ambiguous function assignments discussed in Chapter 11. These latter activities are to do something mundane or strange where the therapist implies (expects) that the client will discover solutions or alternate behaviors or insights that lead to change. One of Erickson's favorite ones was to ask a client to climb Squaw Peak in Phoenix and to wonder about what they would be discovering about him or herself on the climb.

Although we cite Erickson's work here in a book on very brief therapy, it is to be noted that he saw many of his clients long-term. Yet many of his ideas and methods are adaptable to very brief work, especially if you expect that they will work rapidly. It is Erickson's creativity and the immense variety of what he pioneered and practiced that bear studying to give you more variability.

Chapter 10
Jay Haley and Ordeal Therapy

10.1 What is Ordeal Therapy?

In this area of psychotherapy, as in many others, it is evident that Milton H. Erickson either got there first or was the first to develop it into a fine art. This is evident if you read his papers and study his cases. Jay Haley, who was one of Erickson's most astute students, wrote the definitive book on this subject (Haley, 1984). The introduction to this book details the systematics of doing ordeal therapy, and the remainder of the book is replete with many of Haley's intriguing case studies, and a number of Erickson's. Battino and South (2005, pp. 163–8) give a brief description of ordeal therapy, and Battino (2002, pp. 229–44) gives a much longer treatment in a chapter entitled "Ordeal Therapy as Metaphor". The treatment in this chapter is modeled on the material in the last-cited book.

We can begin with two definitions from my unabridged dictionary:

> *ordeal.* 1. A primitive means used to determine guilt or innocence by submitting the accused to dangerous or painful tests supposed to be under divine or superhuman control, escape from injury being ordinarily taken as a vindication of innocence. Ordeals are common to many peoples … 2. Anything used to test character or endurance; any severe trial; a trying experience.

As used in psychotherapy ordeals are closer to the second definition, there being several differences. Although an ordeal may be a "trying" experience, it is not done at such a level as to be dangerous to the client or others. It is not a "test" of character, whatever that may be. And, it is designed for a particular therapeutic purpose. Citing Battino (2002, p. 230):

Ordeals are *tests* whereby a person learns new things about himself. Since they involve the actual doing of a task—living through the ordeal itself, surviving it—the ordeal takes on the character of a living story, a metaphor for that person's life. It is in this sense that an ordeal is a metaphor, the actual acting out in a controlled way of a portion of a client's life. The therapist, rather than some "superhuman" being, is the control agent. There are expectations of learning and change. There is ambiguity, and it sometimes may be difficult to distinguish between an ambiguous-function assignment [see Chapter 11] and a therapeutic ordeal. Ordeals and trials are a continuing part of life, and are the metaphors by which we test ourselves.

While the ordeals of myth and legend are strenuous and generally dangerous, those of psychotherapy are sufficiently onerous to demand the client's attention and challenge their regular and stuck ways of behaving. The expectation—implicit or explicit—is that by carrying out the ordeal the clients *will* learn new things about themselves and discover alternate healthier modes of behavior. The ordeal, in effect, forces the client into challenging alternate behaviors and actions. The end result is usually that the client finds that unique "pot of gold" at the end of the rainbow of their ordeal.

10.2 Haley's Systematics of Ordeal Therapy

Haley (1984, pp. 7–23) lists seven characteristics of an ordeal designed for therapeutic purposes. They are:

1. The ordeal must be more severe than the problem. That is, it should cause more distress than the symptom. If it turns out that the initial ordeal is not sufficient to extinguish the symptom, then it can be increased until it does so.

2. Generally, the ordeal should be related in some way to the symptom, as in the sense of the "punishment" fitting the crime. (On the other hand, totally unrelated ordeals also seem to work.)

3. It is best if the ordeal is something good or beneficial or *health-ful* to the client. These would include activities that the client would like to do (exercise, diet, reading, filing—see examples in next section), but has trouble making the time to do.

4. It is important that the ordeal be something that the client can do within the framework of his health, home, capabilities, and environment. This makes the ordeal something the client cannot legitimately object to in terms of ability to carry out.

5. The basic safety rule is that the ordeal should not harm the client, or other people, or do any damage.

6. For some clients, the ordeal may need to be repeated over a period of time, and the client or the therapist may add appropriate variations.

7. It is crucial that the carrying out of the ordeal be *linked* to the occurrence of the symptom. That is, that on any given day where the symptom appears, that the ordeal must be carried through if at all possible. (Delays should be no longer than 24 hours. Immediate carrying out of the ordeal is preferable, if possible.)

Within his systematic approach, Haley (1984, pp. 7–23) also describes six stages of ordeal therapy, as follows:

1. The problem or concern must be defined in an *operational* way so that both the therapist and the client understand it. When does it occur, under what circumstances, and for what duration?

2. It is essential that the client be committed to getting over the problem. That is, they are ready to work, they are supplying the motivation, and *not* the therapist or some third party. A standard way to "hook" the client is to tell them that there is a fail-safe cure, but that the client will not be told what this is until the client agrees to follow the prescription.

3. The ordeal needs to be selected by the therapist, and this is best done with the client's collaboration and input so it can realistically fit their particular lifestyle. The ordeals need to be behaviorally specific with a clear beginning and ending, and the time, location, activity, and duration need to be clearly spelled out. Written directions are sometimes needed.

4. It is important that the ordeal be described with a *convincing rationale*, i.e., one that is accepted by or acceptable to the client.

5. To be effective the ordeal is continued until the problem is resolved. If there is a physical exercise or component involved, it needs to be sufficiently strenuous so that it can be felt in the muscles the next day. This then provides a kinesthetic anchor.

6. The client's social context must be taken into consideration since neither the client nor the ordeal exist in a vacuum. The therapist then needs some sense about the effect of the loss of the symptom on significant others, the workplace, social settings, etc.

There are thus many factors to consider in using ordeal therapy, and it should not be employed casually. Even so, it can be a significant component of very brief therapy.

10.3 Examples of Ordeals

There are many types of ordeals, and they should be tailor-made for your client and their unique needs. Here are some:

1. *Exercise*—doing some form of exercise that day, that evening, or in the middle of the night. The exercise needs to be sufficiently active so it is felt in the muscles the next day. The exercise can be walking, jogging, push-ups, deep squats etc. An alarm must be set if this is to be done in the middle of the night.

2. *Reading*—this is an opportunity to get that reading done which the client always wanted to do. The reading may be done standing up at 3 a.m. for one hour!

3. *Filing*—this is similar to (2), but can include sorting, pick-up, organizing contents of garage or attic or junk drawer. Doing this in the middle of the night for one hour is good.

4. *House-cleaning*—a particular part of the house is cleaned for one hour at 3 a.m. This is something that the client has continually put off doing.

5. *Writing*—finally working on that paper or dissertation or correspondence or report for one or more hours.

6. *Financial*—doing that long put-off income tax, financial planning, balancing checkbook etc.

7. *Symptom Prescription*—this converts involuntary acts or symptoms into voluntary ones. Involuntary acts include behaviors and compulsions such as: impulsive or compulsive eating or eating avoidance, over-cleanliness or sloppiness, various aches and pains, anxiousness, depression, etc. The ordeal might be to worry for exactly 5 minutes or 30 minutes at some specific time. It can also be to feel as depressed as they possibly can for a specific time period such as 5 minutes.

8. *Two Symptoms*—This is for when a person has two symptoms. One can be required each time the other occurs—this becomes a paradoxical ordeal that effectively works with both symptoms at the same time.

9. *Ambiguous Function Assignments*—Most of the ones written about in the next chapter can be adapted as ordeals. Their ambiguity actually works through paradox.

10. *Ordeals Involving Two or More Persons*—In one of Erickson's cases, he cleverly devised an ordeal for a bed wetting child and his mother. This involved the mother helping him practice his handwriting every morning the bed was wet. However, in order to not miss school, the mother woke up the boy especially early. Both then participated in the ordeal. An entire family can do an ordeal when one member misbehaves. Also, a couple has to go through a shared ordeal when one of them has a symptom that day.

The possibilities of designing ordeals are endless, and you can have "fun" working them out with your clients. Clients generally find ordeals to be intriguing, and it is not difficult to get them to go along once they have been "hooked" into the idea that this special and out-of-the-ordinary idea will help them.

Chapter 11
Ambiguous Function Assignments

11.1 Description of Ambiguous Function Assignments

Milton H. Erickson may not have been the originator of ambiguous function assignments (AFA), but he certainly used them to the great advantage of his clients. However, the most complete description of AFA can be found in the work of Steve and Carol Lankton (Lankton and Lankton, 1986, pp. 136–52). They give the following reasons (p. 137) for using AFA:

Reasons

- disrupts habitual conscious sets

- client will think deeply re: self

- client gives diagnostic information to therapist

- feeling and thoughts both elicited

- client attributes special "magic" to therapist

- client finds some refreshment and excitation about learning

- special rapport is created

- client focuses on any self motivation

- becomes aware of therapy as active

- becomes aware of therapy as something they do

- makes it meaningful

- stimulates a sense of curiosity

- increase sense of therapy's importance

On the same page, they give six indications for when using AFA is appropriate:

Indications

- after rapport and credibility are established
- after resources are built by previous work or for diagnostic purposes
- with clients who have organized conscious minds (not with psychotics)
- when client manipulates or controls therapy
- when client's beliefs about therapy or therapist limit progress
- when client has seen many other therapists without success

An ambiguous function assignment (or ambiguous task) is really a second-order change technique that gets the client to carry out a task in a particularly intriguing and open-ended manner—the therapist implies, directly usually, that the client will learn something of special importance from carrying out the ambiguous activity. In part this is a confusion technique—how can doing this strange thing help me? In part, it is metaphorical since the client is actually living and experiencing in a new way, thus changing the story of their life. (Battino's Chapter 11 (2002, pp. 211–27) is all about AFA as metaphor.) With regard to doing very brief therapy, an AFA is a short-cut for rapid change. What the client discovers can also be considered to be a reframe through changing their perspective about a particular aspect of life.

The Lanktons (Lankton and Lankton, 1986, pp. 142–4) give 8 components of an AFA as follows (quotation marks are used where there is a direct quotation):

1. "Stimulate the client's (or clients') thought about what the assignment will bring, what they will learn, and how it will reveal a therapeutic learning. Use indirect suggestion, metaphor, drama, and contagious delivery to hold interest. The most important aspect is that they have to return to therapy and explain what was learned and speculate why the therapist may have intended for them to have this (unstated) learning."

2. "Deliver with compelling expectancy. The seriousness with which you regard the assignment will necessarily be communicated with your voice tone, facial expression, and other non-verbal delivery." If you are not excited about the potential help of the task and communicate a "compelling expectancy" about helpful outcomes, why should the client be interested in carrying it out?

3. "Be sure to imply that there is or will be value in the activity." Your expectation of value is the compelling reason for asking the client to do something which may appear on the surface to be absurd.

4. "Assign a *specific* task (time, place, act) but *do not reveal its purpose.*" The *general* purpose is learning useful things. But, it is necessary to be ambiguous so the client can discover unique learnings from his own unique experience and background.

5. "Make use of an actual physical object." Examples of this are given in the next section. A physical object concretizes the experience and adds a kinesthetic component. This kinesthetic anchor is important since it provides a direct physical connection to the experience, and adds a touch of ceremonial myth, almost a hero's journey.

6. "Make sure the client is involved in active behavior and not merely fantasy work." It is necessary for the client to actually physically carry out and live through the AFA. They are then in their own metaphor rather than observing it in some abstract manner.

7. "Place binds of comparable alternatives on the client's performance of the task." Would the task better be done in the morning, afternoon, or evening? On a week day, or a week-end day? With this or that object? The bind is that the client is considering how and when to do the task, but not whether or not they will do it.

8. "Maintain 'therapeutic leverage' while utilizing the client's responses.

a. Empathize and reinforce each learning.
b. Identify and accelerate the client's motivation.
c. Do not accept the client's initial thinking as complete.
d. Continue expectancy and imply the existence of more information.
e. Challenge or stimulate the client to do the continued thinking.
f. Continue the above until therapeutic receptivity is maximized."

When doing AFA work it is important to keep all of these components and their rationales in mind. The difficult part is to get the client sufficiently interested to actually carry out the AFA. Remember, that it is your expectation that they will learn something of benefit when they do the AFA. In the follow-up session, the client reports back on what happened while doing the AFA, and in thinking about it afterwards. That is, the client needs to process the activity in their own way.

11.2 Some Suggestions for Ambiguous Function Assignments

There are many possible AFAs, and you need to match the assignment to your client and their needs. The material in this section is based on Battino (2002, pp. 217–20), and briefly lists possible activities. They can be adapted to couples and families. Be sure to add sufficient detail as to time of day, location, duration of activity, physical effort involved, number of times to repeat activity, whether to involve someone else, when and how to report outcomes, and safety.

1. *Carry an object*—The client is told that carrying a particular object on their person for a given period of time will be useful. The object can be in a pocket or a bag or hand-carried. It might be to carry a moderately heavy stone around the block they live on three times every day. The object usually has some weight or bulk so that it is inconvenient to have with them. The object can

be significantly symbolic or totally irrelevant since the value of this exercise is for the client to supply meaning to the activity.

2. *Climb something such as a hill, peak, or mountain*—Erickson frequently had people climb Squaw Peak in Phoenix. However, any readily available high place within the client's physical capability is all that is needed. It may be to go part way up this height. It may be to climb the stairs up a twenty storey building, rest, and return down the stairs. The client is to think about what this means to them. They may carry along a significant (or insignificant!) heavy object or written message, leaving it at the top or reading it aloud. If they take rest stops, you can ask them to think about what this rest means for the rest of their lives. Again, they supply the significance of the activity—what did that crazy therapist think I was going to find out here? (Since safety is always an issue, it may be important on certain climbs to have a companion along.)

3. *A walk in the woods*—Recalling Robert Frost's poem "The Road Not Taken", the client can be requested to take a walk in a safe wooded area, stopping at each place the path branches, and debating the merits of taking one path or the other. Which path is the "right" one for them at this time (even though it may be the "left" branch!). How is their life "branching"?

4. *Shopping malls*—What will they discover about themselves by spending some time in a shopping mall as an acute observer of the people there and the stores and their contents? In studying the variety of couples and families who pass by while you stay in some fixed place, what do you notice about them? What would it be like to change places with one of them? Following someone unobtrusively and walking and moving as they do, what is it like to be in someone else's shoes/footsteps?

5. *Bibliographic AFAs*—You give the client a particular poem/essay/article/book/chapter/children's story/magazine/Bible passage to read. Ask them to wonder why you gave them that to read. Why that author or reading or writing? What did they discover for themselves?

6. *Random reading*—This is connected to (5), but involves opening some book such as the Bible, an encyclopedia, a dictionary or an anthology to a random page, reading something on that page, and then wondering about the special significance of what they have read. Art books are also useful for this exercise.

7. *Museums and zoos and botanical gardens*—The client visits one of these places and then is asked to wonder about why this particular place? What is special about it? What connection does what they observe there have with their concerns, and how will this visit help them?

8. *Web browsing*—The client is given a specific topic to browse on the web, and they are then to follow whatever links make sense. Where did they get to? How much is there to learn?

9. *Blind or deaf walk*—Sighted and hearing people can learn much from safely doing a blind or deaf walk. In fact, this can be done in any location by closing your eyes for a few minutes, or putting on sound mufflers. Walking carefully around a familiar room with your eyes closed can be eye-opening!

10. *Write a letter*—There are iconic figures such as Santa Claus, Jesus, God, a professor of a particular subject, a guru, Buddha, the Dalai Lama, a historical figure, or a fictional character that you can write a letter to. In the letter you tell this person exactly what you need to lead a satisfying life, and that you just wanted to share this information with them. As a follow-up, you could then write a letter to yourself imagining how they would respond.

11. *Random walks*—If you were to safely do a random walk in your neighborhood or in a city or in a museum or in a zoo or in a department store, what would you learn? Where do your feet take you? Where do you end up?

12. *Amusement park or circus*—Visit an amusement park, circus or county fair and discover for yourself some special significance in the rides, performances, events, exhibits, sideshows. Did the therapist have something specific in mind when this was suggested?

13. *Symptom prescription*—Pick a symptom that you wish to know more about or to change. Do it in a different place, at a different time, in a different way, and/or for a different duration. How has this changed you and/or the symptom?

The object of an AFA is to get the client to do something—generally out of the ordinary—and to wonder about the significance of that activity. What have they learned? What does this mean? What has changed? Again, it is the therapist's expectation that the client will discover something useful in this exercise that makes it potent. Your imagination is the source of AFAs.

Chapter 12
Burns's Nature-Guided Therapy

12.1 What is Nature-Guided Therapy?

In my many years of experience in working with people who have life-challenging diseases, there appear to be some common responses when they are confronted with the diagnosis, and are forced by that diagnosis to re-evaluate their lives. The diagnosis generally implies a shorter life span. In addition to all of the decisions that need to be made about medical treatments and the practical matters of finance and jobs, there arise the existential questions about the meaning and goals of life. If the medical prognosis is just several more years of life, then how should you live out your remaining time? What are the things that are really important? It is not the new car, the promotion, or serving on some committee. Invariably, I have found, there are two things that stand out for a person at that time of setting priorities. The first is people and relationships, loving and being loved, touching and being touched, being with loved ones, and sharing in their lives. Life, apparently, is with people, in the humanity of contacts and relationships. We might guess that a large part of this is that when a person is very sick that they regress to childhood states seeking the comfort of parental love and care. You just cannot survive such catastrophic times alone, without others.

The second thing that assumes great importance is contact with Nature, with trees and flowers and sky and grass and clouds and woodlands and prairies and mountains and flowing water and the ocean. This may, perhaps, be the most primitive of our instincts—returning to the earth in which we are rooted. Beds and chairs need to be sited so that the person can look outside, at least be in visual contact with the world around them. In a hospice facility I know of, every room has a large window looking out on a bird feeder and shrubs and trees. There is also a duck pond nearby, and ducks and geese freely wander the grounds. When possible, if the patient or family request it, the patient is bundled up in a bed or a wheelchair and taken outside for a while. Nature is important. There have even been studies showing that patients in hospital rooms that have views of nature appear to heal faster (Jerstad and Stelzer, 1973; Lowry, 1974; Ulrich, 1984).

George W. Burns (1998) in his book entitled *Nature-Guided Therapy: Brief Integrative Strategies for Health and Well-being* has written about how to use contact with Nature in psychotherapy. He also calls this approach *ecotherapy* or *ecopsychotherapy*. He writes about his terminology as follows (p. 20):

> In some ways the term *nature-guided therapy* expresses well what this approach is about. It defines nature as an initiator of health, healing, and well-being. By health I mean a state of physical wellness. … Healing is the process of rectifying an imbalance of the state of health. It is about fixing a problem or resolving a disturbance to our normal state of equilibrium. Well-being I define as a broader concept than either health or healing. It takes into account the emotional, relationship, and spiritual needs of the human species. Well-being thus includes a state of physical health as well as a mental and emotional state of consonance. Well-being is attained when a person is experiencing an inner state of wellness, exists in a healthy environment, and experiences a harmonious connection with that ecology. … The term *nature-guided* also includes a sense of gentleness. …

Although Burns prefers the term *ecopsychotherapy*, throughout his text he also uses the shorter term *ecotherapy*. He states (p. 135):

> The basic premise of ecotherapy is simple: Contact with the natural environment can and does bring about changes at cognitive, behavioral, affective, and physical levels. Simple exposure to natural stimuli can result in rapid change.

In his introductory chapter, he lists ten characteristics of ecopsychotherapy: (1) effective; (2) brief; (3) solution oriented; (4) client focused; (5) pragmatic; (6) wellness based; (7) motivation enhancing; (8) encouraging of choice; (9) empowering; and (10) enjoyable.

These ten items are explained and justified in some detail, with literature references. For example, with respect to being brief he cites (p. 23): "Ulrich et al. (1991) have shown that a range of psychophysiological indicators of stress can be brought back to baseline levels within 4 to 6 minutes of exposure to videotapes of wilderness environments." This, of course, is quite remarkable. And, with respect to ecopsychotherapy being solution oriented, Burns states (p. 25):

> The therapist's expectations may also provide the model for the client's expectations. If the therapist assumes that a solution is possible, that change can and is likely to take place, and that such change can occur rapidly, then those assumptions will almost certainly be communicated to the client and even adopted in a manner that will determine a successful and rapid outcome.

It is encouraging to find another therapist stating the thesis of this book!

12.2 Some Ecotherapy Procedures and Examples

Burns's Chapter 3 is about "sensual awareness", although I would use the more neutral term of "sensory awareness". Burns writes rather poetically about how he helps clients create multimodal sensual experiences *in vivo* (p. 55):

> The combination of multiple sensual experiences is not a simple formula like $1 + 1 = 2$. In fact, it is more like $1 + 1 = 22$ or 102. For example, if we stand in front of a waterfall, electromagnetic radiations are being inverted through our cornea in waves, striking 130 million receptors before being communicated via the optic nerve to the visual center of our brain. Sound waves are funneled into auditory chambers reverberating through drumlike skins and the body's tiniest bones before being transmitted along neural pathways and communicated to the auditory centre of the brain. But what we experience may be a sense of ecstatic awe.

The perfume of a loved one inhaled by one of our 23,000 daily breaths is scanned by 10 million olfactory receptors capable of detecting approximately 10,000 different odors. Add the caress of that person's finger on the back of a hand, detected by cells of our tactile receptors as a pressure signal. When the waves of electro-magnetic radiation from the candle on the dinner table strike the cornea, the response may be an overwhelming sense of love and passion.

The senses are extremely powerful in evoking emotions and memories. This is particularly the case with odors since the sense of smell connects with a primitive part of the brain.

To help a client access in useful ways their sensory experiences, Burns has developed a "sensual awareness inventory", or SAI. This is reproduced here and may be used freely as long as attribution for the inventory is given to G. W. Burns.

Sensory Awareness Inventory

Under each heading, please list 10–20 items or activities from which you get pleasure, enjoyment or comfort.					
SIGHT	SOUND	SMELL	TASTE	TOUCH	ACTIVITY

(Used with permission of George W. Burns. Burns, G. W. (1998). *Nature-guided therapy: Brief integrative strategies for health and well-being.* New York: Brunner/Mazel.)

Burns found that in his experience the majority of stimuli listed under each heading were nature-based. This is remarkable. He also found that there appeared to be a dissonance between what the clients list as pleasurable and what they actually do! He states that the SAI is primarily designed as an awareness- and action-oriented inventory, rather than as an inventory for assessment. The SAI is usually presented to the client at the first session. Administration of the SAI involves three steps (p. 68–9):

1. Ratifying *what* learnings were gained from completing the inventory.

2. Determining *how* those learnings can be used for continuing therapeutic gains.

3. Determining *when* those learnings can be put into practice.

Thus, the SAI helps the client discover what it is that is important to them. The therapist then explores with the client ways in which these "discoveries" can be useful, and helps pin down just when those particularly helpful activities will be carried out. For example, four "when" questions that Burns poses are (p. 69):

- *When* can you start to do those things for your ongoing pleasure?

- *When* will be the first opportunity you'll have to (for example) spend some time in the garden, listening to the birds and smelling the boronia?

- *When* will be a convenient time each day to pause and enjoy one of the pleasures from your list?

- *When* would you like to begin to feel a little happier?

Remember that the items in the SAI are those generated by the client, and are therefore particularly meaningful to them. The therapist provides guidance *and* permission to carry out these activities. In my experience in using the SAI, I have also found that most of the entries are nature-related. In times of psychological stress (why the client has come to visit you!) connecting with nature is just as important as in times of physical health-related stress. We cannot underestimate the power of a flower, a cloud, a blade of grass, a raindrop or a snowflake.

Sensate focusing is the subject of Burns's Chapter 6 (pp. 87–98) and is a technique for helping the client tune into and be aware of sensations of pleasure, comfort, and wellbeing. Focus shifts from the unpleasant and undesirable to the desirable.

The heart of ecotherapy may be considered to be nature-based assignments, and these are approached by Burns in a variety of ways in several chapters. (He also gives many illuminating case histories along the way.) The assignments involve interacting with nature in some way. It is helpful, as in AFA, for the assignments to contain a level of ambiguity that the client fills in in their own unique way while the assignment is being carried out, and afterwards in thinking about it.

- I am not sure what you will discover for yourself when you take the time to observe three moonrises and three sunsets this coming week.

- Spending some time by the bank of that stream and carefully studying the motion of the water and the water insects and the interplay of light and shadow can be surprisingly useful.

- Walking in the rain without an umbrella, and taking your rain hat off from time to time to really experience the rain can be special for you.

- Just take the time to carefully watch a group of clouds moving and changing shape, and just wonder about the shape of things.

- On your next walk in the woods pick up an interesting stone, a leaf, a twig and a piece of bark. Enjoy their forms and textures.

- When you are next at the seashore/pond/woods/waterfall/back yard, and at different times of the day or night, close your eyes for five minutes and just listen and smell and touch.

Natural ordeals have already been covered to a certain extent in Chapter 10. There are many possibilities, and it is always useful to add ambiguity to these ordeals.

In Chapter 13 on ecotherapy for enhanced relationships, Burns gives several useful exercises:

> *Exercise 13.1:* Discuss the things you and your partner enjoyed doing together in your courtship, especially when they involved contact with nature, such as walking hand in hand at the beach, parking at a scenic spot, or picnicking in a national park. Together, select a time to recapture one such experience. Then do it. [P. 173.]

> *Exercise 13.2:* Study your partner's Sensual Awareness Inventory and note the things that bring him or her pleasure. From your observations, select an experience that will pleasure your partner. [P. 181.]

> *Exercise 13.3:* Study, along with your partner, each other's Sensual Awareness Inventory. Explore your common themes of enjoyment. Discuss how you could engage in an experience of mutual pleasure. Form a plan of how to practically do so. Put the plan into practice. [P. 182.]

> *Exercise 13.4:* As a family, complete Sensual Awareness Inventories. Allocate a mutually convenient time to discuss the scales. Focus on the family's common themes of pleasure, ensuring that each member's needs are addressed. Plan the time and means to create a mutually pleasurable activity or activities. [P. 184.]

12.3 Nature Heals

Contact with and involvement with nature can be and is healing. It is basic, fundamental, organic, rooted, natural, ecological and spiritual. Burns has elucidated for us the many ways that nature-guided therapy, ecotherapy, can be beneficial. Take a walk and smell a flower and touch the bark of a tree and take a deep breath and feel the warmth of the sun and the coolness of a breeze and listen to the wind in the treetops and waves breaking and re-connect and re-new yourself.

Chapter 13
Metaphoric Approaches

13.1 Uses of Metaphor

This author has written about the uses of metaphor for psychotherapy and healing in *Metaphoria: Metaphor and Guided Metaphor for Psychotherapy and Healing* (Battino, 2002). (Please consult the first chapter of that book for a brief guide to other relevant books on metaphor. Amongst other items, there is a chapter on language for metaphor, and another on the delivery of metaphors.) This chapter will use that book as its main source of material. After some introductory material, Kopp's *Metaphor Therapy* (1995) will be discussed, followed by Battino's "Guided Metaphor" (2002).

In therapeutic practice, metaphors are, in effect, stories told by the therapist, and those stories contain within them ideas and suggestions designed to provide the client with choices for change. From childhood on, stories have an universal appeal, capture the listener's attention and imagination, and can be entrancing. Within the framework of doing very brief therapy, metaphors can provide a shortcut to rapidly changing the client's perspective (reframing) about what it is that is disturbing them, or about where they have been stuck. Since a metaphor is heard on both a conscious and an unconscious level, the client has the opportunity of processing information on both levels and finding ways to change from the inside out, as it were. We may even posit that it is the unconscious or inner mind that latches onto metaphor-initiated possibilities of changing behavior, and then comes up with its own unique and individual solutions derived from those possibilities. The significant part of this work is what the client does with the stories you tell, rather than your intentions. This means that the metaphor needs to be sufficiently *vague* about *many* intriguing possibilities. Battino's book (2002) and the many references cited therein are rich sources for therapeutic metaphors, as are Erickson's writings and tapes.

The four elements of a basic metaphor are: (1) gather information; (2) construct the metaphor; (3) deliver the metaphor; and (4) arrive at some kind of closure. In gathering information you listen to the client's presentation of their concerns. You also gather information about the client's background, interests, hobbies, and so on, so that the metaphor can fit within the framework of the client's experience. The metaphor is constructed to be somewhat isomorphic with the client's concerns and the outcomes you would like the client to consider. The word "somewhat" is deliberately used to indicate that the metaphor needs to be more *parallel* to the client's concerns rather than an exact replica. Subtlety is needed here, because if the protagonist in the metaphor is easily identified as the client, then the client would most probably feel manipulated rather than simply interested in the story. (A list of ideas for metaphors is given in the next paragraph.) The metaphor is delivered using your best story-telling technique—this involves variation in voice, pace, emphasis, etc. Also, within the metaphor you can *embed* particular words and phrases and ideas, and *mark them off* with your delivery. If this is done subtly within the delivery, then it is primarily the client's unconscious mind which is listening and processing. Adding some elements of mystery, drama, and suspense is useful. The closure re-orients the client to the present time and place, and may contain a "punch" line or theme or moral.

Some themes that can be built upon for basic metaphors are:

- A visit to a guru or wise person.

- A hero's journey with its obstacles and mission.

- Constructing a building of some size for some purpose.

- Weaving cloth with all of the variants of thread and pattern.

- Baking bread or preparing food using a recipe or free-style.

- Sailing with attention to the wind and the waves, to the boat and the goal.

- Growing corn, planting a tree, a flower or a vegetable.

- Using well-known children's stories such as the Three Little Pigs.

- Traveling in foreign lands or interesting environments.

- Planning an activity such as a trip.

It is useful to read and study published metaphors, and to have available a repertoire of your own basic stories that you can adapt. Initially, you can write out your metaphors or record them.

13.2 *Richard R. Kopp's Metaphor Therapy*

The "traditional" way of using therapeutic metaphors was for the therapist to create or adapt a metaphor for a particular client. These were then therapist-generated metaphors. Kopp (1995) reasoned that client-generated metaphors would be more specific to the client's needs, and developed Metaphor Therapy based on that paradigmatic shift. In the introduction to his book, Kopp makes a number of relevant statement (page citation in parentheses):

> The theory of Metaphor Therapy rests on the proposition that individuals, families, social groups, cultures, and humanity as a whole structure reality metaphorically. [P. xvi.]

> The theory of Metaphor Therapy also proposes a neuropsychological explanation of the brain mechanisms that mediate mental (linguistic and cognitive-affective) metaphoric structures and processes. [P. xvii.]

> Metaphor Therapy advances the view that metaphor is central to the process of change in psychotherapy and is not related to any single approach or method. [P. xvii.]

> Metaphors are mirrors reflecting our inner images of self, life, and others. [P. xiii.]

> It is suggested that Metaphor Therapy integrates the view that cultural myths are the narrations by which our society is unified and the view that personal myths revealed in one's earliest childhood memories are the guiding fictions that unify an individual's personality. [P. xxii.]

> [an epilogue] … presents Gregory Bateson's (1979) view that mind and the evolution of all living things in nature are unified within a single principle, 'the pattern that connects,' and that the pattern that connects is metaphor. [P. xxiv.]

Kopp discusses doing metaphoric work in two broad categories. The first involves exploring and transforming the client's metaphoric language, and the second involves exploring and transforming the client's early memory metaphors. The latter category, of course, is psychodynamically related. In Battino (2002, pp. 170–6) are presented some alternative simpler ways to do Metaphor Therapy, and they are briefly presented here (please read Kopp's book for a full appreciation of his work, and Battino's book for more detail on the alternative methods).

13.2.1 Client-generated Metaphors for Immediate Concerns

1. *Discovering the metaphor*—This is primarily done by listening to the client talk about their life, and *listening* for life metaphors. One way of eliciting such information is to ask a question such as, "Suppose you could describe what your life is like now as a story or a fairy tale or a myth, what would that be? Can you give me some details?"

2. *Enlarging the metaphor*—Once you have some sense of the client's metaphor, you can explore the dimensions of the metaphor to obtain a sufficient amount of information. Questions such as the following can be asked: "Describe what is going on; describe what that feels like; what is going on around you? what would I notice if I were there with you?"

3. *Transforming the metaphor*—The "transformation" is really a modification of the de Shazer et al. "miracle question" (see Chapter 6). Questions to ask are: "Suppose you could change in some simple and easy and realistic way so as to be more comfortable with yourself, how would you change that? Suppose that a miracle occurred right now and you could change [the metaphor]—what changes would occur so that you

get what you want? What are the things that would be different in your life if this miracle occurred?"

4. *Ratification of the changed metaphor*—After the previous step it is useful to ratify and consolidate the changes in the "transformation." "How will this have changed your life? How will your life continue with its new possibilities? What will you be doing differently?"

13.2.2 Transforming the Early-memory Metaphor

1. *Accessing the early-memory metaphor*—This involves a regression to the past where the client recalls significant event(s) related to their present-day concerns. "Thinking about what it is that is troubling you today, and drifting back in time to your earliest childhood memory about that, what comes to mind? This is something specific that happened to you as a child. When you have that memory firmly and clearly in mind, please let me know by nodding your head or saying 'yes'. Thank you."

2. *Experiencing that early-memory metaphor*—"At this time, experience that earliest memory just enough, safely, to let you know that it is really connected to your present-day concerns. Let me know that by nodding or saying 'yes'. Thank you."

3. *Transforming that early-memory metaphor*—"Since that earliest memory in some way contains the origins of your present-day concerns, would it be okay to just change that memory to what you would have liked to have happened instead? That memory can start out the same way, and you can change it and adjust it so that you get the ending you prefer, especially when you look back. When you have changed that memory to your satisfaction, please nod or say 'yes'. Thank you."

4. *Returning to the present with changes*—"Good. Now, please return to the present, noting how the changed ending of that earliest memory has already changed other memories, and how you feel and think about yourself at the present time. Note the specific changes that have occurred. When you have finished doing this, please nod or say 'yes'. Thank you."

Kopp has provided a useful paradigm shift in how to do metaphoric work, and it needs to be carefully studied. There are, of course, many more details in his book.

13.3 Guided Metaphor

With the impetus of Kopp's work, and incorporating many other approaches such as guided imagery, narrative therapy, solution-focused therapy, and Erickson's hypnosis and hypnotherapy, Battino (2002, pp. 177–91) developed an approach he calls "Guided Metaphor." Since he uses guided metaphor with about one half of his clients, and finds it to be quite effective for brief therapy work, details of the method are given in this section.

The basic idea is that everyone has and is a story. You get the client to tell their own story in a brief form—such as one-half of one page—which you copy down. This is then condensed to one sentence, and then distilled to a word or two or a phrase. The client is told that they can edit or rewrite their own life story as they wish it would have happened. They tell you this new story, condense it to a sentence, and distill it into a word or two. They then tell you how this new life story will have changed their life, and provide you with some details. Finally, you tell them back their old story, the new story, and the changes they have told you. In essence, you are *guiding* them through the metaphor of their life and the changes *they* select for it. This is their story.

There are six steps as follows:

1. *Opening*—This is an introduction and explanation of the importance of everyone's having a life story that they tell themselves and others. Life stories have beginnings, middles, ends, themes and key episodes.

2. *Elicitation of client's "old" life story*—Ask for the client to tell their life story in a one-half page summary. Then, ask the client to condense that old life story into one sentence; and then distill it into a word or two or a phrase.

3. *Elicit the client's "new" life story*—This is elicited by saying something like the following: "Assuming you had the power of an editor to change your life story so that it would be as you would have liked it to have been from the perspective of the present time, what would that new life story be? Please condense your new life story into one sentence, and then distill that into a word or two or a phrase. Thank you."

4. *Elicit how the new life story has changed their future*—Suggested language for this is: "Considering your new life story to be true, how will this have changed your future? Please be explicit about the changes. Thank you."

5. *Delivery of the client's personal life metaphor*—Now tell the client back their old life story, their new life story, and how the new story has changed their future. Use your notes so you can accurately quote the client's language.

6. *Ratification and reorientation*—Ratify by some ideomotor signal such as head nodding that they have indeed experienced these changes in their story, and the effects of those changes on their life at this time. Then compliment them for the courage to do this work, and reorient to the present time.

Clients readily follow the guided metaphoric procedure. This is a kind of "global" life change process where they talk about their life and the changes in it. When telling the client about their life and its changes, it is useful to use hypnotic language forms and patterns. Generally, the client goes into some level of trance during this re-telling. Sometimes it is useful to ask to hold the client's hand at the point where you shift to the new life story. The "old" story is usually about twice as long as the "new" story, yet in the re-telling you should reverse this and spend about twice as much time telling them the new story and its future as in the telling of the old story. And the more details you can pile on about the new story and its future, the better. This detail makes the new story and future more real and probable. The whole process takes 30–40 minutes.

It is also possible to do the guided metaphor approach as a writing exercise. Details for this are given in Battino (2000, pp. 188–91). In fact, in presentations on the subject, Battino has the audience do the guided metaphor individually in writing, and then asks for a volunteer to demonstrate the process with the re-telling.

Chapter 14
Rossi's Rapid Methods

14.1 Fail-safe Methods

Ernest L. Rossi has pioneered many areas in hypnosis and hypnotherapy. He was an early collaborator of Milton H. Erickson's, and edited his collected works, in addition to publishing several books with Erickson. (You can find an up-to-date bibliography of his works at his web site: www.ernestrossi.com, as well as many of his articles which are freely available for downloading.) In recent years, he has been interested in neuroscience and neurogenesis. In part, this interest has been involved with searching for connections between brain function and hypnosis, and also for providing a theoretical basis for hypnosis in chaos on nonlinear dynamic theory. He has a wide-ranging mind and is a first-class scholar. With respect to the focus of this book, Rossi developed a number of "fail-safe" rapid change methods. A number of them will be discussed in this section. He collaborated with the late D. B. Cheek, the master of ideodynamic methods, and those methods will be presented in Section 14.2.

The earliest and, perhaps, the simplest fail-safe method that Rossi developed is what he called the "moving hands" approach. In his book entitled *The Symptom Path to Enlightenment: The New Dynamics of Self-Organization in Hypnotherapy: An Advanced Manual for Beginners* (Rossi, 1996), he writes about this in terms of four basic accessing questions with respect to inner healing (pp. 194–5). In essence, in the generalized form, Rossi developed a simple and elegant four-step model for doing psychotherapy:

1. Establish that the client is ready to do meaningful work on some particular concern.

2. Have the client do an inner search of all of the material relevant to that concern.

3. Have the client review all possible options for solving that concern realistically.

4. Ratify with an ideomotor signal that the client is going to use one or more of those options.

It is difficult to conceive of a more efficient way of working. In using moving hands, he provides a physical anchor for each step of the process.

The language I use (based on Rossi's work) for these four steps are:

Rossi's Moving Hands

1. Please hold your hands comfortably in front of you, and about eight to ten inches apart. [client is sitting] When you are ready to work on whatever concern brought you here today, will you find those hands moving together all by themselves to signal yes? [Wait until the hands move close enough together to touch before moving on.]

2. Thank you. Now, will you find one of your hands and arm drifting down all by itself as you carry out an inner review of all of the relevant factors relating to that concern? [Wait until that hand touches the client's lap.]

3. Thank you. At this time you can internally review all of the realistic options for solving and resolving that concern in the best manner, while your other hand and arm drift down all by themselves. Take whatever time you need, knowing just how fast your mind can work. [Wait until that hand touches the client's lap.]

4. Thank you. When your inner or unconscious mind knows that it will be using those useful options in your daily life, will you find your head nodding "yes" all by itself? Thank you.

There are, of course variants in language that can be used for different purposes. The client can be moved along in the process by appropriate gentle comments. If the client has gone into a trance state during the process, you need to re-orient them to the present at the end of step 4. The process is "fail-safe" in the sense that once the client positively responds to the first step, the other steps naturally follow. For the first step you can also say, "If there is another concern which is more important, will you find your hands drifting apart all by themselves?" Then, for step 2 you can say, "With respect to this other concern, will you ... ?" The entire procedure takes about 20 minutes. It occasionally needs to be repeated. It is client-specific and an example of "secret therapy" in that the client does all of the work within their head, and they generate all of the solutions and motivation. The therapist is simply the guide and facilitator.

Rossi ties in these four steps to his overall framework of change (using hypnosis) as:

1. Data collection: initiation, sensations.

2. Incubation: indication, arousal, feeling.

3. Illumination: insight, breakout, intuition.

4. Verification: reintegration, thinking.

These patterns are discussed in great detail in the first part of his 1996 book and also on p. 214 et seq., which can be consulted for more information.

Rossi uses the therapeutic double bind in his Box 5.5 (1996, p. 207), converting the basic accessing questions in the following interesting ways:

If your inner mind is ready to deal with that issue ...

Will those hands move together all by themselves to signal yes ...

Or will they move apart all by themselves to signal no ...

Until a more significant question comes up privately in your mind?

If your hidden self wants to explore that problem privately ...

Will those eyes close all by themselves to signal yes ...

Or will they remain open ...

Until a deeper problem comes up that you need to deal with first?

If your symptoms [pain, anxiety, depression or whatever] are really related to the personal problem(s) you associate it with …

Will those symptoms momentarily get better …

Or worse for just a moment or two as a signal that something is changing …

Will those eyes close more or less all by themselves so you can explore the source and solution of that whole problem deeply within yourself?

This is conscious carefully constructed language chosen to move a client along, while providing the confusion of using double binds to ensnare them in the process.

In Figure 7.1 (p. 245), Rossi presents a "hands polarity" process based on his four stages. With the client seated comfortably, the stages are:

Stage 1: Initiation—Sensations—If you are ready to do some inner work on that problem will you place your hands palms up as when you are ready to receive something? As you focus on those hands in a sensitive manner, I wonder if you can begin to let me know which hand seems to experience or express that fear (or whatever the negative side of the patient's conflict may be) more than the other?

Stage 2: Incubation, Arousal—Feeling—Wonderful, now I wonder what you experience in your other hand by contrast at the same time? Good, as you continue experiencing both sides of that conflict will it be okay to let me know what begins to happen?

Stage 3: Insight, Breakout—Intuition—Interesting? Something changing? And is that going well? Is it really possible?

Stage 4: Reintegration—Thinking—What does all that mean to you? How will your life be different now? How will your behavior change now? What will you do that is different now?

This is an example of polarity work, and also an excellent example of Rossi's minimalist approach in asking simple questions based on his careful observation of the client to move the process along. Also, notice how his questions are clearly expectational of change.

In *The 20-Minute Break* with D. Nimmons (1991), Rossi explores the idea of *ultradian rhythms* in everyday life and in psychotherapy. They write about this (p. 12):

> The ultradian performance rhythm is a widely varying pattern alternating between 90 and 120 minutes of activity with 20 minutes of rejuvenation. There are wide variations among people and situations in the timing of these rhythms. They shift easily to help us adapt to the changing demands and circumstances of the real world.

If people do not allow themselves the time to experience these ultradian rest periods, then they may experience "ultradian stress". It is important to pay attention to these natural cycles.

The second edition of *The Psychobiology of Mind-Body Healing* (Rossi, 1993) was much expanded over the first edition. Its first section deals with the psychobiology of mind–body communication, and the second with the psychobiology of mind–body healing. Both sections are thoroughly researched and referenced. There is a central theme of mind–body interactions on physiological and neurological levels, and that these interactions can be influenced by hypnosis and other approaches to bring about significant physiological changes such as enhancing the immune system. This book contains 15 "teaching tutorials" which are condensed interventions using mind–body work.

Rossi's book entitled *The Psychobiology of Gene Expression* (2002) is a well-researched volume on fundamental discoveries in current neuroscience and how this affects the way we understand human nature, as well as methods for using these ideas to help clients. For example, it is possible to enhance neural growth in the brain throughout one's life (neurogenesis) via the three processes of enriching life experiences, novelty and physical exercise.

To complete this summary, I must mention Rossi's latest book (2005) *A Discourse with our Genes: The Psychosocial and Cultural Genomics of Therapeutic Hypnosis and Psychotherapy*. This remarkable book brings up-to-date research results in the field. A brief quote from p. 36 gives some of the flavor of the book and Rossi's wide-ranging scholarship:

Consciousness can turn on gene expression, synaptogenesis, neurogenesis, and mind-body healing!

Rossi's Chapter 9 (pp. 201–41) contains a variety of his therapeutic approaches based on his theories.

In closing this section, I should mention how Rossi works in a minimalist mode with certain clients. In the 2002 book, Chapters 7 and 8 are devoted to a detailed description using a transcript of a session before a large audience with a client named Celeste that was audio and videotaped. Celeste had rheumatoid arthritis in her hands, and at the end of the session was moving her hands freely. (The videotape is available from the Milton H. Erickson Foundation, IC-92-D-V9.) This tape needs to be carefully studied to follow how Rossi uses minimal statements to move the client along.

14.2 Ideodynamic Methods (mostly D. B. Cheek)

In our environment there are a great many responses that we give automatically. These are ones that occur outside of consciousness, or were not willful conscious responses. Some common ones are shaking hands and stepping on the brake when you are a passenger in a car. These automatic responses are also called *ideodynamic* responses. They can be used for doing effective brief therapy. LeCron (1964) was probably the first popularizer of this method. Cheek and LeCron (1968) have been the main proponents of this technique, and their book gives many examples of the use of the Chevreul pendulum—any small weight attached to a string, held loosely in the fingers, and free to move. They also discuss finger signals. Rossi and Cheek (1988) describe using ideomotor signals for the resolution of many problems. Probably, the best book in this area is the comprehensive treatise by Cheek (1994). Chapter 10 (pp. 281–305) in Battino and South (2005) is on the application of ideodynamic methods in hypnosis.

The method as refined by Cheek uses finger signals where one finger is designated as the "yes" one, a second as the "no" one, and a third as the "not ready to answer now." (If the third finger denoted "maybe", it would be the most frequent choice!) It is assumed that the fingers are under the control of the inner or unconscious mind. This assumption also holds for the Chevreul pendulum where micro-muscular movements move the pendulum. It is further assumed by practitioners that "the body never lies", that is, that you can really trust these unconscious responses.

In effect, as refined by Cheek, using finger signals is like playing the game "twenty questions" with the fingers giving one of their three responses. Please note that "unconscious" finger movements are generally small and erratic—conscious movements are smooth and larger. Although it is not indicated below, it is useful to say "thank you" after each finger response to let the client know that the movement has been observed. Also, assume "yes" answers where appropriate to continue the questioning. In addition to the finger signaling, you can also ask for brief verbal responses. The sequence might be something like the following:

1. I am going to say "yes", "yes", "yes". Please let your "yes" finger respond by moving. [Repeat for "no" and "not ready to answer now". You can also ask a series of questions with obvious answers like, "Is your name Mary?" "Is today Tuesday?"]

2. Is there a particular concern you are ready to work on at this time?

3. Let us assume that this started at some time in your past. Did it start before you were twelve? [This is repeated until a year is picked by the client.]

4. Was there more than one such initiating incident?

5. Would it be okay to spend a brief amount of time safely reviewing what happened then? [Yes] Please do so and let me know by lifting your "yes" finger when you have completed that brief safe review.

6. You know that you are a different person now with much experience since that time back then. Knowing what you know now about yourself and your life, would it be okay to be completely and safely over the effects of that time? [If "no", then ask, "Is there something getting in the way of doing that? ... Do you know what you need to do to get past that, or to nullify it? Please do that now.]

7. Is there anything else you need to do about what has been troubling you? [If "yes", then proceed in a similar manner to the preceding.]

8. Having successfully dealt with what started all of this in your past, would it be okay to move forward to the present time, comfortably, noting what changes this has made for the good in your life? Thank you.

A typical ideomotor finger session lasts about 20 minutes, and the effects appear to be permanent. Please note, again, that it is the client who is really doing all of the important work internally. It is reassuring to clients to have their fingers do all of this "talking", and it provides a physical anchor for the entire process.

In Rossi and Cheek's book (1988) there are many "boxed" sets of instructions using ideomotor methods for particular conditions. As some examples, Box 14 is on "Accessing and reframing memories from surgical anesthesia", Box 18: "Direct healing suggestions in emergencies", Box 20: "Ideodynamic healing of burn injuries", Box 24: "Accessing and facilitating inner sexual resources", and Box 27: "Resolving sleep and dream issues". This book is a wonderful resource for healing and psychotherapy.

14.3 Some Concluding Comments

In this chapter, we have skimmed over the contributions of E. L. Rossi in terms of rapid methods of working with clients, and also the work of his colleague D. B. Cheek on ideodynamic methods.

Both the "moving hands" approach and ideomotor finger signaling are used frequently in my practice. Clients find them to be intriguing, and learn a great deal about themselves by using these internal methods. Of course, it takes some skill and practice to use these methods.

Chapter 15
NLP Approaches

15.1 The NLP Meta-model of Language

Neurolinguistic Programming or NLP was developed by Richard Bandler and John Grinder. The literature on NLP is vast, so I will only cite here the original two volumes that started the field, and two further books which offer additional practices. The first two books, on the "structure of magic", are by Bandler and Grinder (1975), and Grinder and Bandler (1976). They are still worth studying, and are of particular interest to this section since they introduced the Meta-model of language usage. The recent books by Bodenhamer and Hall (1999) and Hall and Bodenhamer (2003) entitled *The User's Manual for the Brain*, Volumes I and II, contain extensive NLP information and interventions in sufficient detail for a practitioner. The bibliographies therein will lead to other relevant sources, yet those two books are a sufficient resource for interested readers.

Bandler and Grinder originated the NLP Meta-model of language, indicating that it arose from asking the question: "The client says something—how do you know what to say next?" Since Grinder is a linguist, they turned to linguistics for their answer to that question and adopted the terminology of Chomsky's Transformational Grammar model. Their initial analysis proposed that people tend to talk in "surface structures", that is, their communications are "incomplete" with respect to the experiences they are talking about—the "deep structure". A "deep structure" sentence would be linguistically more complete in terms of communication. Bandler and Grinder's model analyzed language with a view to eliciting from the client more exact communication using a series of focused questions. They identified three main classes of language usage that could lead to stuckness: distortions, generalizations and deletions. Bodenhamer and Hall (1999) in their Chapter 8 (pp. 135–74) give a thorough presentation of the Meta-model, along with suggestions for extending it. Whereas we can consider good language usage in hypnosis to be "the precise use of vague language", within NLP we can think of the Meta-model as being "the precise use of precise language". This section then contains a brief review of the three main classes of the Meta-model. Please read the two *User's Manuals for the Brain* and other NLP books if you are interested in pursuing this subject in more detail.

15.1.1 Distortions

1. *Nominalization*—A nominalization is the result of converting an action or process word (verb) into a static event or thing (noun) or a judgment into a description or assessment (adjective). In effect, nominalizations have deleted large amounts of information by concretizing a process. Within the framework of psychotherapy, we can consider all diagnoses to be nominalizations, that is, a person has depression/anxiety/panic attacks/phobias/OCD and so on, or can be described as depressed/anxious/panicked/phobic/obsessive-compulsive etc. Because such nominalized descriptions (by self, or worse, by professionals) tend to become self-fulfilling and limiting they need to be challenged by recovering the associated activity. Ask, "How are you depressing yourself?" rather than, "Describe your depression."

2. *Mind Reading*—This occurs when we think we know what is going on in another person's mind *and* what it is that is motivating them. Mind reading statements need to be challenged by asking the person what is actually going on in their mind.

3. *Cause-Effect*—The client believes that something a person has done causes a particular response, as in "You make me sick"—the other person somehow "forces" this upon you. Typical cause-effect words are: *make, if … then, then, because, as you.* "Because of you, I must …" Again, challenge the process: "How does X cause Y?"

4. *Complex Equivalence*—Bodenhamer and Hall (1999, p. 147) state:

    We generate a complex equivalence whenever we use a part of an experience (an aspect of external behavior) to become equivalent to the whole of its meaning (our internal state). Thus when we become aware of the external cue, we then assume the meaning of the whole experience. "You did not tell me that you love me this morning; you just don't love me anymore."

The client connects this with that without questioning the connection.

5. *Presuppositions*—Bodenhamer and Hall (1999, pp. 149–50). These are conceptual and linguistic assumptions that have to exist in order for a statement to make sense. Presuppositions are not stated directly; in language they work indirectly, covertly, and unconsciously. They are founded in the person's belief system about themselves, about life, existence and so on, and can tell us much about the person's model of reality. Such presuppositions are similar to mind reads but refer to self. In therapy, they can work as suggestions (see section 4.2 above).

15.1.2 *Generalizations*

1. *Universal Quantifiers*—These are words and statements that make universal generalizations such as: "I'm always late", "Men never listen". This sense of absoluteness in the belief of the client severely restricts their choices. Typical words are: *all*, *never*, *always* and *none*, and they can be challenged by repeating the word back to the client in a questioning tonality: "Always?"

2. *Modal Operators of Necessity and Possibility*—This mode of thinking puts limitations on the client's model of the world through the use of words such as: *should/should not, can/cannot, possible/impossible, am/am not, will/will not, must/must not, can't, ought/ought not, have to, need to,* and *it's necessary*. They proscribe behavior: "I can't do it." "I should do it." "That's impossible." These beliefs, for that is what they are, can be challenged by: "What stops you?" or "What would happen if you did/didn't?"

3. *Lost Performative*—A lost performative belief/statement is a value judgment in which the speaker or source of that judgment is not named, i.e., missing from the statement. Examples are: "Boys shouldn't cry." "Girls need to be polite." "It's not good to be too strict/happy/sad/successful/open." Can you hear a relative saying that ...?

15.1.3 Deletions

1. *Simple Deletions*—These occur when the speaker/client leaves out information about a person, thing, action or relationship. Examples are: "She hurt me." "I feel scared." "I really don't know." For the first statement, a response might be, "Who hurt you in what way?"

2. *Comparative Deletions*—In this pattern, a person makes a comparison, but leaves out the specific persons, items, or things compared to whatever standard the person has in mind. Words used in this pattern are: *best, most, better, more, less, most, least, worst.* "She is just so much better off now."

3. *Lack of Referential Index*—The referential index is the person or thing that does or receives the action from the verb in the statement. This pattern involves using pronouns such as *they, nobody, one* and *this* which are nonspecific. "They did a terrible thing." "The ones who did this ..." "Nobody cares a hoot anymore."

4. *Unspecified Verb*—These are verbs that describe vague and nonspecific actions: *injure, upset, hurt, care* and *concern.* "Who specifically hurt you and in what way?"

NLP practitioners have been superb in analyzing language usage, and in working out ways to assist a client be more precise in communication. Gaps in a client's perception of the world are demonstrated by the language they use, and these gaps can be filled in by helping the client fill in what was missing. Linguistically, getting a client to change from "I can't" to "I won't" has a profound impact on how they think about themselves and what they do. You can't change if you do not have choices, and these language patterns help the client to find more choices. The Meta-model of language can be quite useful in particular situations, especially since it provides you with a host of responses so that you know what to say when the client says ...

On pp. 40–61, Hall and Bodenhamer (2003) list 20 presuppositional attitudes that are central to NLP work. They are:

1. The map is not the territory.

2. People respond according to their own internal maps.

3. Meaning is context-dependent.

4. Mind and body are systems that inevitably and inescapably affect each other.

5. Individual skills are developed and operate as we enhance and sequence our representational systems.

6. We pace another's sense of reality by respecting and matching the person's model of the world, creating rapport.

7. We distinguish person from behavior because we are more than our behavior.

8. In some context every behavior is useful and has value; every behavior is driven by some positive intention.

9. Behavior and change should be evaluated in terms of context and ecology.

10. We cannot not communicate—even when we try not to communicate, we do.

11. The meaning of communication is in the response we get.

12. Whoever sets the frame for a communication exchange governs things.

13. There is no failure, only feedback.

14. The person with the most flexibility exercises the most influence in the system. [Law of Requisite Variety.]

15. There is no resistance, only the lack of rapport.

16. People are not broken: they work perfectly well. [People have all the internal resources they need.]

17. People can learn quickly, sometimes with one experience.

18. It is better to have choice than no choice, and the more the choices, the more flexibility in handling the challenges of life.

19. People make the best choices available to them when they act. [People are not their behaviors, nor do their behaviors define them.]

20. We are responsible for "running our own brains" and thereby managing our own states.

15.2 The "Swish" Method

The word "swish" was applied to this method as the change was supposed to happen as quickly as you would say, "Whoosh." It is effectively an internal visualization technique wherein the clients substitute a more desirable picture or image of themselves for a present-day stuck concern or belief that can be represented by an image/picture. The process uses "submodalities", which can be defined as the qualities and characteristics of the ways (modalities) that people use to represent physical or emotional states or beliefs. It is suggested in the NLP literature that people tend to "represent" their experience primarily in one of three sense systems: visual, auditory, and kinesthetic (the senses of smell and taste are generally far less relevant). That is, one person "sees", another "hears", and a third "feels". These primary senses are the modes or modalities. The submodalities are the variable characteristics of that sense. For example, auditory submodalities would include: pitch or frequency, tone, volume, rhythm, location, single or multiple source, tempo, intelligibility, melody, duration, and whether it is music, noise or voice. These variants "color" (visual) the modality and give it dimension.

The way I use this technique is based on Chapter III in Andreas and Andreas (1987, pp. 37–59). They state that the three major elements of the swish are (p. 37):

1. Selecting the cue to swish from.

2. Developing a desired self-image that is attractive and motivating.

3. Using powerful submodality shifts to link the two together.

The cue image begins the swish and should be something that is always there just before the problem behavior occurs. This cue image can be external or internal. If it is an external real-world one, then it should always be associated, that is, connected in some way to the client. An internal image needs to be exactly as the person experiences it when it produces the unwanted response. The desired self-image is something like who you are when you have more choices and the unwanted behavior or response is not a problem. This desired self-image should be dissociated, i.e., not connected to you, but out there so that you are drawn towards it.

To begin, the client is asked to think about something mildly uncomfortable like a body ache or a touch of sadness. Then they are asked to imagine how that sensation would change if a picture or image of it: came closer, moved further away, grew larger, grew smaller, was in full color, was in black and white, had a frame around it, tilted toward or away from them, and moved or was still. They are then asked how these variations changed their response— did the mild uncomfortable sensation become stronger or weaker or stay the same? These questions *calibrate* the client's way of perceiving these changes. The cue image is about the present state which they wish to change. The desired self-image is of themselves as they would like to be with respect to this particular concern. Once these two images and the client's strongest change submodalities are known, then they can be linked together.

Have the client experience/visualize the cue image. Then, within that image in some small area, have the desired image appear. It is better to have the desired image replace the cue image in two or more submodalities (such as getting closer and larger simultaneously) than one. The swish is always from the cue to the desired image. This internal imagery work is repeated five or more times, blanking out that internal screen between each swish, and goes faster each time, until the cue image can no longer be held.

The "swish" is a rapid way of changing the client's internal imagery of who they are and how they respond to a particular difficulty. It needs practice, of course, and studying the Andreas and Andreas chapter cited above would be a good beginning.

15.3 *Time Line Therapy*

James and Woodsmall (1988) have developed a way of doing therapy based on time changes that they call "Time Line Therapy". Woodsmall has written about this separately (1989). Bodenhamer and Hall (1999) have a long chapter (pp. 353–81) on using time within the NLP framework. This section is based on the work of James and Woodsmall.

Their thesis is that how we store memories affects how we experience our lives, and how we experience time. Generally, people store memories in time within their minds in a linear fashion. "Through time" is a Time Line that stretches from left to right or right to left in front of you. An "In Time" one stretches from front to back and goes through you. Most Anglo-Europeans represent their memories in the "through time" mode, and left to right.

The following is a guideline for doing Time Line Therapy based on the authors (James and Woodsmall, 1988) outline on p. 87.

1. Find out if the client is in Through Time or In Time so that you know which language to use to guide them along their time line.

2. Ask them to float above their time line in some safe way.

3. Find out which submodalities they use for representing their experiences in the past, present and future. They should be the same for all. If not, change them so they are the same brightness and approximate color—the future can be slightly brighter than the past.

4. Have them go back in time to the past while they are safely floating above their time line to find the earliest unwanted experience in the chain of what they wish to change in the present.

5. Observing those past memories safely, have them preserve whatever learnings are present in them in some special place that they reserve for those learnings.

6. Have them change the critical memory or memories to what they want them to be, or just have them remove those memories. Reassure them that this can be done safely.

7. If memories were removed, replace them with favorable ones. This can be done using the swish technique or by direct suggestion that this is possible.

8. Continue steps 4–6 using those earliest relevant memories until the unwanted memory, state or behavior is not longer accessible.

9. Since it is safe to do so, have them float down back into their time line and follow it to the present, noting whatever changes have occurred by the work they have done in their past.

10. Have them go out into their future (left or right) and look back to now noticing how their life has already changed, and what the changes are.

Time Line Therapy can be used in a relatively short session for: memory removal, changing events (in the past), deleting negative emotions (by "unhooking" them from the time line), removing phobias, installing a compelling future, and changing the direction of the timeline by changing the organization from Through Time to In Time or vice versa. This is an interesting approach that is related to Section 15.6 on changing personal history.

15.4 V-K Dissociation

NLP practitioners have developed an interesting technique for the rapid removal of phobias. This procedure is flexible and can be adapted to many concerns since it is possible to conceive of, let's say, something such as anxiety or panic or obsessive/compulsive behavior, as being a phobia. The V-K dissociation model for working with phobias is based on the premise that the client sees something in their environment which recalls an event which triggered and triggers that phobia and in recalling that event they experience all of the anxiety, stress and tension of the original phobic inducing event. The process works in "breaking" the connection between the initiating visual (it could be olfactory or kinesthetic or auditory) experience and the kinesthetic physiological reaction. Bodenhamer and Hall (1999, pp. 117–21) give directions for carrying out this process. Their directions for the "fast-phobia cure" (pp. 121–2) follow in abbreviated form:

1. Establish a resource anchor.

2. Acknowledge to the client the mind's ability of one-trial learning.

3. Imagine a blank movie screen. The client imagines being in a movie theater where they can see on the screen before them a black-and-white photo of themselves *just before* the onset of the bad memory, and at a time when they still felt safe and secure.

4. Next, the client dissociates once more from their body and moves into an imaginary projection booth. They can now look out of the projection booth at themselves sitting in the theater and observing that black-and-white picture of themselves up on the screen.

5. Now, the client runs a black-and-white movie of the bad memory or phobia all the way through to the end of the event, watching themselves watching the movie.

6. Once the client runs the movie to the end to a scene of comfort/security, ask them to freeze frame and white-out or black-out the picture so they see a blank screen.

7. Now, lead the client to associate into the screen where they blanked out the movie. They leave the projection booth and enter their body in the theater seat; then they enter the movie and associate into the image that appears on the screen. Have them associate into the image of themselves at the end of the movie *after* they have survived the trauma or phobia.

8. Direct them in running the same movie backwards, in color and associated. Once you have established that they have done this, have them run that same movie backwards again, associated, and in color in one or two seconds. You can anchor them to a sound like "whoosh" to this rapid re-run.

9. The client now repeats steps 7 through 8 until the kinesthetic response disappears. Be sure they clear the screen after each re-run.

10. Test and future pace by seeing if the client can access the phobic state. If the phobia response reappears, you may re-run the phobia cure.

This procedure requires skill at language usage and practice, but it has been the author's experience that it really works, and results in permanent cures.

15.5 Reframing the NLP Way

This procedure is described briefly in Bodenhamer and Hall (1999, p. 359) and is the subject of a complete book by Bandler and Grinder (1982). This has also been called six- or seven-step reframing or parts reframe, and is different than "ordinary" content and context verbal reframing. The procedure assumes that there is a "part" within you that is taking care of you in some way by keeping some painful memories buried deep in the unconscious mind. Bodenhamer and Hall write about this as follows (within working with time lines) (p. 359):

> Your protective part keeps these memories hidden from the conscious mind. Sometimes the conscious mind creates unconscious parts to repress painful memories so as to consciously, but not

realistically, deal with them. Thank the part for protecting you all those years. Assure the part that you have now reached the age and wisdom where you can accept those painful memories in order to deal with and transform them. Tell the part that you have other ways of protecting yourself. Assure that part that it will not be destroyed and the purpose to us is to allow it to accomplish its highest intent for you. Get in touch with this part that no doubt believes it is protecting you and ask it its intent/purpose for you. When you get an answer, ask it what that answer's intent/purpose consists of for you. Continue asking this question until you get an intent/purpose that will give you permission to go back and clean up the old memories. [Then go back in time and clean up those old memories.]

15.6 Changing Personal History

This pattern is interesting since it connects with the guided metaphor approach in which the client has the opportunity to change their life history, i.e., the story of their life. Since memory is malleable and affected by all of one's experiences, it is open to being altered. The changing personal history approach is a direct way of doing this. The following is adapted from Bodenhamer and Hall (1999, pp. 271–4) where two versions appear.

1. *Access a problematic memory*—From the client a problematic, unwanted, or unpleasant feeling is accessed. An anchor is placed for this.

2. *Do a transderivational search (TDS)*—Use the anchor to assist the client in finding an earlier experience with this same feeling. Establish the age at which this occurred, and anchor this state.

3. *Continue the TDS*—Continue using the anchor to have the person go back in time and find several other related or similar experiences, and establish the age at which each occurred.

4. *Break state*—Have them return to the present and find a resource that would help them in that past situation to have coped better and more effectively. Anchor this resource state.

5. *Collapse anchor*—Then, have the person return to the *earliest* experience as you fire off both the resource state anchor and the negative state anchor *simultaneously*. "How does this resource change that past memory and what you felt like then?" "How would this resource make that past different?" And then have them come up through their personal history, stopping at each (negative) past experience with the resource anchor and note how their history begins changing through time so that each experience becomes satisfying. [Emphasis added.]

6. *Trouble-shooting*—If it turns out that the client has difficulty in changing the past experience, have them return to the present to access and anchor whatever additional resources they need to carry out this change work.

7. *Break state*—After they have changed all of the past experiences, have the client break state. After waiting a short time, have them think about that problematic feeling.

8. *Test*—Have the memories and feelings changed, and in what ways? Do they have an internal sense about the presence of their resource(s)?

9. *Future pace*—To anchor these changes for the future, have the client think about similar experiences that may occur in the future, knowing that they will have their resource(s) with them.

As with most of the NLP interventions and patterns, there are many variants available in the literature. You can adapt them to your own style and clients after you have had some experience using "standard" approaches.

15.7 Summing Up

NLP practitioners have made great contributions to the language of therapy in their systematic studies and classifications and illustrations. They have also been most prolific in devising effective, efficient and interesting psychotherapeutic strategies and interventions. The ones in this chapter are those that I use most frequently. Recall the "principle of requisite variety", which states that in any complex interaction, the component with the most variability controls. That component can also be the most effective.

Chapter 16
Narrative Therapy

16.1 Introduction

Narrative Therapy has many elements that are helpful in doing very brief therapy. It was developed by White and Epston (1990) who wrote the seminal book in this area. Two other books by them that are useful to read are Epston and White (1992) and White (1995). The book by Freedman and Combs (1996) is an excellent introduction, and well-worth studying, and the book edited by Monk et al. (1997) provides much practical information and case studies. O'Hanlon (1994, p. 28) states that narrative therapy has at its heart, "… its fierce belief in people's possibilities for change and the profound effects of conversation, language and stories on both therapist and client." On p. 23, O'Hanlon continues about Third Wave Therapists (he characterizes narrative therapists as being part of a "third wave" in the history of therapy),

> … a willingness to acknowledge the tremendous power of past history and the present culture that shape our lives, integrated with a powerful, optimistic vision of our capacity to free ourselves from them once they are made conscious. Third Wave approaches talk to the Adult Within.

This is powerful stuff. Battino (2002, pp. 265–74) gives a brief introduction to narrative therapy as it relates to metaphoric work. In this chapter we present some of the aspects of White and Epston's work as they are incorporated into the author's very brief therapy approach. For a more complete sense of this approach, please read White and Epston (1990), and Freedman and Combs (1996). It is also worthwhile noting that White and Epston proceeded in their work from a grounding in social, linguistic and communication theory.

16.2 *Some Elements of Narrative Therapy*

White and Epston (1990, p. 83) give the following as being part of a therapy working within the narrative mode of thought:

1. privileges the person's lived experience;

2. encourages a perception of a changing world through the plotting or linking of lived experience through the temporal dimension;

3. invokes the subjunctive mood in the triggering of presuppositions, the establishment of implicit meaning, and in the generation of multiple perspective;

4. encourages polysemy ["polyphonic orientation"] and the use of ordinary, poetic and picturesque language in the description of experience and in the endeavor to construct new stories;

5. invites a reflexive posture and an appreciation of one's participation in interpretive acts;

6. encourages a sense of authorship and re-authorship of one's life and relationships in the telling and retelling of one's story;

7. acknowledges that stories are co-produced and endeavors to establish conditions under which the "subject" becomes the privileged author;

8. consistently inserts pronouns "I" and "you" in the description of events.

A basic tenet of Narrative Therapy is the credo: "The person is never the problem; the problem is the problem." This rather simple statement contains a great deal of wisdom. First, it gets away from the medical model with its limiting diagnoses of a person has and is this or that. The person is unique and individual, and at this point in time has some concerns that are providing difficulties in their life. So, let us deal with the problem or concern and not label the person as some dysfunctional entity that needs to be repaired by following some predetermined protocol. Erickson, for example, found dealing with symptoms, i.e., their removal, to be effective. This could not be the case *if* the client was the problem.

Narrative Therapy's credo is the basis for their most well-known technique: *externalization*, which is one that is quite useful in doing very brief therapy. O'Hanlon quotes the Canadian therapist Karl Tomm as saying (O'Hanlon, 1994, pp. 24–5):

> Ironically, this technique [externalization] is both very simple and extremely complicated. It is simple in the sense that what it basically entails is a linguistic separation of the problem from the personal identity of the patient. What is complicated and difficult is the delicate means by which it is achieved. It is through the therapist's careful use of language in the therapeutic conversation that the person's healing initiatives are achieved. … What is new about the narrative approach is that it provides a purposeful sequence of questions that consistently produce a freeing effect for people.

The narrative therapy approach relies on a careful use of language and a sophisticated series of questions which are designed to generate experience rather than to gather information. Freedman and Combs (1996, pp. 113–43) provide a systematic development of the use of questions for this work, along with many illustrations.

Battino (2002, pp. 269–70) writes about externalization:

> The process of externalization—with a person or a family—begins with coming up with a mutually acceptable *name* for the externalized problem. Are you being controlled or tricked by: Anger, Fear, Depression, Paranoia, Anxiety, Urine, Fatty Food, Bulimia, Panic, Anorexia? How long has this been going on? Have there been times when you were able to resist _____? put it in its place? ignore it? tell it off? This linguistically separates the person from the problem label, and clients soon perceived their problem in this externalized way. To aid in this separation the ogre or demon is made more real by attributing to it evil intentions and tactics. This is a nasty entity who has it in for you, and who has made your life a misery in many ways—elicit those ways from the client.

Battino (2002, p. 271) continues:

> If the person is not the problem, and the problem is the problem, then separating the person from the problem via externalization is an essential step in moving from what the client considers to be involuntary, unable-to-control behavior to voluntary and

controllable behavior. Narrative therapists cleverly personify the controlling element to make it real in an as-if sense. … Once the problem has been externalized, then in a solution-focused-brief therapy sense *exceptions* to being controlled are sought. These exceptions, times when the "demon" has been thwarted or resisted, are the basis for the client's new life story, that is, the new story is built on the client's proven strengths and resources. "What will let you continue to ignore/thwart/overcome/restrict Depression (for example)?" "What can you do to put Depression in its place so it will no longer bother you?"

So, the externalization frees the client from being the "bad" person, and opens up the possibility of creating a new life and life story free of these external controlling influences. (An interesting speculation here is how this procedure may be related to exorcisms!) I have found the externalization process to be particularly effective with children and teenagers—they appear to be closer to the imaginative world that helps here.

Narrative therapy grew out of much work with families, particularly in rural settings. It is no wonder then, that this work is very social-context- and family-oriented. Except for the therapist's office, people live and function in a social context of family, friends, work, local culture, religion etc. Whatever new story is developed needs to be acknowledged and ratified by this social network. This is described as "creating an audience for perceiving the new identity and new story". One way of doing this is to have the client proclaim in a public letter or document that they are now free of Depression (for example). This document/letter is frequently prepared by the therapist.

Letters are used in a variety of ways and quite extensively in narrative therapy. White and Epston (1990, pp. 77–187) devote an entire chapter to this. The following types of letters are well illustrated in their book, and this list is adapted from Battino (2002, pp. 271–3):

1. *Letters of invitation*—These are used to engage or entice people to enter therapy or to continue in therapy. The tone is respectful and courteous, and generally involves "hooks" that are connected to externalizing the problems in the client's life.

2. *Redundancy letters*—Since people get stuck in roles that they feel they cannot give up, a redundancy letter is designed to show the client that he is no longer needed (redundant) in a particular role. The roles may be: supermom, parent-watcher, sibling protector, marriage protector, family problem fixer, sex object etc. This kind of letter evolves from knowledge of the client's situation.

3. *Letters of prediction*—David Epston writes (Epston and White, 1992, pp. 94–5), "Often at the end of therapy I ask permission to make my predictions for a person's, relationship's, or family's future. I regularly use the period of six months as my time-frame. I often refer to this time-frame as 'your immediate future.' I post these predictions in 'letters,' folded and stapled, with 'private and confidential' prominently displayed on them, along with 'Not to be viewed until _____ date in six months' time).' My intentions in doing this are twofold: (1) the prediction proposes a six-month follow-up/review, and suggests that this would be an interesting exercise for both the person/family and therapist to undertake; and (2) since it is my suspicion that most people won't wait but will review their review prior to the specified date, then I expect that the prediction will function as a prophecy which may fulfill itself."

4. *Counter-referral letters*—These are letters of referral that emphasize the development in a narrative sense and refer to the externalization so that the referral person has a sense of the client's accomplishments and change vis-à-vis the problem.

5. *Letters for special occasions*—These letters ratify comment on the special occasion and ratify progress.

6. *Brief letters*—Brief, reassuring letters, that connect to people who are relatively socially isolated.

Under the category of brief letters are letters on: past session thoughts; therapist needs help; non attendance; recruiting an audience; mapping of influence (to show progress); historicizing; challenging the techniques of power; challenging specifications for personhood and for relationship; that reminds me!; chance meetings.

The types of letters above are just a sampling of the variety of letters that narrative therapists routinely use in their practice. One typical use is sending a letter after every session—these letters serve as case notes, reminders to the client(s) of what has happened in the session, ratification of change, predictions of future behavior, and a way of continuing contact and maintaining rapport. People are so addicted to the mail, and the special power of letters, that letter receiving takes on extra significance in their lives. I have found that sending letters after a session is quite effective. At the minimum, the client has something in hand to testify to what they did during the session.

Battino (2002, pp. 273–4) lists some additional narrative therapy practices that he has found to be useful:

> Clients can be asked to record their own stories via a wide range of media: videotape, audiotape, testimonial letters, in various genres, the telephone, and personal letters. The narrative structure is conventionally that of a success story. Narrative therapists also make creative use of certificates. These are printed in certificate format. One example is a certificate entitled, "Monster-Tamer and Fear-Catcher Certificate," and states, "This is to certify that _____ has undergone a Complete Training Programme in Monster-Taming and Fear-Catching, is now a fully qualified Monster-Tamer and Fear-Catcher, and is available to offer help to other children who are bugged by fears." These certificates are dated and signed by the therapist. … Diplomas are also awarded.

For these certificates and diplomas, a stock of special paper is maintained.

16.3 Summing Up

The reader at this point may feel somewhat frustrated in that in this chapter and the previous ones there is just an overview of the many things a therapist may do. Without making this book onerously long, the material is meant to indicate what this author does, and the many different approaches that he has available to him in doing very brief therapy. Of course, he has studied these methods in depth, and urges the reader to do the same with those that particularly fit your style. The more choices you have, the more choices your clients have. In a given session, even the open-ended ones the author uses, there is only time for a few separate interventions. In many cases the session may just be a kind of wide-ranging reframing chat that ends with a brief hypnosis period. Narrative therapy, with its useful paradigmatic changes, is always a probable choice.

Chapter 17
Rituals and Ceremonies

17.1 Introduction

The book on rituals and ceremonies is the one by Hammerschlag and Silverman (1997)—it is worth reading and studying for all of the information and examples in it. They do make a useful distinction between rituals and ceremonies, although many people use these two terms interchangeably. *Rituals* are *routine* activities such as habits in the sense that they are repetitive and part of everyday life. We all have morning "rituals" in terms of the order we do things: shower, toilet, dress, and whether you put items of clothes on with left or right limbs first. The sequence of these events is ritualized, and the activities within the events are also generally fixed in sequence. The activities tend to be unique and individual. Some may be related to a particular spiritual or religious practice, as in reciting morning prayers. Rituals are *ordinary* activities.

On the other hand, *ceremonies* are *special* events and have a connection to the spiritual or sacred or religious. For example, getting married, graduating from school, being baptized or circumcised, a memorial service, an initiation, an inauguration, and burning your divorced spouse's love letters are ceremonies. Ceremonies are designed to give meaning to special occasions. All religions have their own traditional ceremonies for the end of life memorial service, internment, and mourning. Within a given religion these activities are prescribed and therefore ritualized, but the totality of the special events surrounding death is a ceremony.

Since rituals are routine, it is ceremonies which are more connected to psychotherapeutic work. Ceremonies can be structured to accommodate life transitions, symbolize changes in perspective and outlook, and ratify behavioral changes such as stopping smoking and controlling weight, for example. Life transitions are a basic part of everyone's life story. In a sense, we live from ceremony to ceremony, each one a special marker on our life's journey. Within the framework of psychotherapy, a ceremony can be created to effect or mark a significant change in a client's life.

Ceremonies typically incorporate the following elements:

- leader(s) to facilitate
- specific goal
- significant or sacred object
- group of select people
- particular site
- mutual respect/reverence
- special timing
- specific order of service or components.

A wedding ceremony, for example, involves: a priest, rabbi or minister; religious and/or civil legalities; wedding ring(s); family and friends of those wedding; a church, synagogue, temple or other space that takes on a sacred significance; an exchange of solemn vows (in modern times those who frequently design their own service and statements); a particular date; and an order of service prescribed by their beliefs.

An example of a ceremony is the Navajo Talking Circle used by Navajos and other Native Americans. Generally, these are ceremonies designated for healing purposes, whether physical or mental or spiritual. There is a person who is the focus of the circle. There is a leader who facilitates, and who explains the goal of the meeting. It is usually the focal person who provides an object sacred to them which is passed around the circle. You may talk only when you are holding the object. When you finish talking, you pass the object on to the next person until all have had a chance to speak. The rules are:

- whatever is said and shared in the circle is confidential and may not be repeated outside of the group

- each person talks about their own *personal* experience, from their heart, for as long as they wish

- when they finish, the next person has the attention of the group

- there is *no* cross-chatter, interruption, or commenting on what others have said

- everyone listens attentively and respectfully to whoever is speaking

Generally, each person speaks only once. Time permitting, and if it is appropriate, a person may speak again for themselves. Non Native American groups may dispense with the use of a sacred object and just go around the room, or permit a random order of speaking. A key factor that Hammerschlag points out is that in Native American tradition when you "speak from the *heart*", you are considered to be speaking the truth. The expectation is for heart-felt personal statements rather than intellectual commentary. Thus, it is personal stories which are shared. This sharing is healing.

Germane to this chapter is Remen's story, "Making Caring Visible", in *Kitchen Table Wisdom* (1996, pp. 151–3). In this segment, she gives details about a healing circle that is designed to prepare a person for surgery or radiation or chemotherapy. The following is taken from Battino (2002, p. 323):

> The group usually consists of a few family members and close friends, and is convened solely for this purpose. The meeting is a few days or a week or so before the surgery or the beginning of the treatment. The central person brings along a small stone that is symbolically important to him. The stone should be flattish and no larger than an inch or so. The rules are explained, the central person does not speak, but hands the stone to a person seated next to him.

> In this, Navajo Talking Circle rules apply. The person holding the stone tells a personal story about a trauma or difficult time in his life. Then he describes what personal characteristics, attributes, or actions helped him through that time. These could be courage, strength, faith, love, persistence, belief in a divine being, stubborn-ness, prayer. This personal tale is concluded with, "I put *love* and *prayer* into this stone so you may have it with you." The stone is passed on. In this manner each person ends with a similar statement, endowing the stone and imbuing in it his or her way of

coping and surviving. When all have spoken, the stone, which is now the repository of all of these personal gifts, is given to the central person. He would tape the stone to a hand or foot, and inform the medical staff about its sacred significance.

This ceremony has been used by Remen for over twenty years with much success. She has received positive feedback from area surgeons. Ceremonies can be life-saving and life-enhancing.

17.2 Psychotherapeutic Uses of Ceremonies

Ceremonies can be part of a therapeutic treatment plan. A recent client had troubling dreams which woke him at night, after which he rarely went back to sleep. The ceremony we developed was for him to place a number of objects which were symbolic for him about the troubling aspects and population of the dreams into several small caskets he bought at a Halloween store. He then buried these in his back yard. The process brought him some relief for a number of months. (Not all ceremonies are completely successful upon execution!)

The psychologist S. Gilligan (1987, pp. 177–95) has written and lectured on helping his psychotherapy clients through critical points in their lives by using ceremonies. The ceremony is part of the treatment protocol.

When a marriage or long-term relationship breaks up, the "survivor" may be helped to put the experience behind them by burying or throwing out symbols that maintained connections with the relationship. Symbolic and real objects may be burned, buried, crushed or removed in some way. The ceremony becomes a physical anchor for leaving the old feelings and dependencies and memories behind. "With this ring I thee do wed, and with this trash I thee do forget and move on." The ceremony in some sense becomes a kind of exorcism that can be used to rid your soul of unwanted demons.

Grief can be shortened and made easier with various rituals and ceremonies. The planting of memorial trees or shrubs or flower beds can be helpful. Memorial funds help; also, the donating of clothes and other personal objects helps others while removing reminders.

For those who have life-challenging diseases ceremonies can be especially helpful. Indeed, they can be used for resolving unfinished business, ending old and unneeded feelings and attitudes and habits and relationships, marking a new phase of life (you are alive until that last moment), and for celebration of the end of a series of chemotherapy or radiation treatments. Religions have ceremonies for the last period of life, and they are important for religious people. For others, ceremonies can be devised for the end of life time, that last transition, which are special for the person involved. I have participated on a number of occasions in helping people in their last stage of life design their own memorial service, shaping the ceremony by which they wanted to be remembered.

In concluding this brief chapter, it only needs to be pointed out that ceremonies help us partake of the sacred, and that life changes and transitions are indeed beyond the ordinary.

Chapter 18
When All Else Fails

I vividly recall attending a conversation hour at one of the Erickson Congresses where the speaker was one of my heroes in the field. This was a man who was literate and creative and who had made a significant impact on the development of psychotherapy in the last century. Someone in the audience asked how he worked with alcoholics. This icon's response was a direct, "I never work with them." It was said with such finality that there could be no mistaking him and no follow-up. I turned to the man I was sitting next to (Scott Miller), and we both stared at each other with incredulity. How could someone of this man's stature and experience utter such a statement? Perhaps, to our naive minds, we had bought into the myth of omniscience and omnipotence that frequently surrounds psychotherapists, particularly famous ones. If this man would not work with alcoholics, was there any hope for me working with that group? Or, for that matter, was there any hope for alcoholics? (There certainly were positive answers to both of these questions for Miller (see Miller and Berg (1995).) Yet, this man's response raises some important issues (see below).

Milton H. Erickson is another hero, and if you read his case studies and the unbelievable range of clients he worked with, and the remarkable successes he had with such unusual people, you must wonder about the first man who wouldn't work with alcoholics, and also wonder about the possibilities and probabilities of helping the people who come to see you. Therapists, of course, tend to write about their successes. Thus, it is difficult to uncover places where people such as Erickson failed, or turned away clients they felt they could not help. If you carefully read the Erickson literature, you will find quite a few mentions of clients he turned away. There is generally an accompanying statement that he felt he could not help them. Were they too resistant? And what does "resistance" mean?

NLP practitioners are fond of saying that there is no such thing as a resistant client, there is just a therapist who does not know what he or she is doing. This is certainly an upbeat statement in the sense of always having hope that you can help clients. There is also a certain amount of hubris in this statement, since the inference is that NLP practitioners always know what they are doing, and have an almost infinite variety of interventions at their beck and call—*they* always succeed. (I would hasten to add that *all* self-respecting therapists have that feeling at some time!) Having written this, I would add that it is important for your clients to believe that you feel that you can help them. It is also useful to have many strategies for helping clients, and to be sufficiently flexible to create new strategies and/or alter old ones. Is it possible to create a new therapy for each client? No. But, it is possible to be flexible. For the rest of this chapter I will write briefly under various headings about what I do "when all else fails".

Ask the Client

A favorite "trick" that Gestalt therapists were taught was to switch roles with the client when you got stuck. "You know, I'm having trouble figuring out what to do that will help you. Since you know yourself and your circumstances much better than I possible can, let's switch roles. You be the therapist, and I'll play you as best I can. Okay?" So, you do that. When "playing" the client it is helpful to use their own words and descriptions, and to *exaggerate* some of the problem behaviors. (You do not exaggerate to the point of bur-lesquing them.) This role reversal gives the client the opportunity to "see themselves as others see them", and to get an external perspective on their behavior. Many clients are so wrapped up in their own concerns that they lose perspective, perceiving the world solely from within. Of course, the therapist acting as client can be as "resistant" as necessary!

A more direct approach is to say, "I'm stuck. Do you have ideas or guesses as to what it is that we can do together that will help you?" ("Guess" is an important word here.) "What do you think/feel will help?" "You know, in a way, I am searching for a miracle to help you because I am all out of ideas now. What 'miracle' is going to change your life the way you want it to change?" The ball is thrown over into their court. This is a useful tactic to use with "therapist killers" who have a great variety of successful experience thwarting therapists. If you just "give up" on them, where else do they have to go but within themselves for help? This is done with empathic support—you really want to help them, but ... There is a danger here in that the client will simply walk out; so be it.

De Shazer and his colleagues write about three kinds of clients: (1) customer—a person who is there to obtain help for changing and is ready to work; (2) complainant—a client who is not sure about really wanting to change, but is open to being persuaded that it might be useful; and (3) visitor—the client who (generally) has been forced to be there and is not interested in change, but is interested in getting someone off their back by going through the motions. There is usually nothing you can do with visitors, a fair amount you can do with complainants, and much you can do with customers. In every case, however, all can be asked directly about what they think will help them.

Listen

It is a truism when working with people who have life-challenging diseases that the single most important thing you can do for them is to *listen*. Rather than be concerned with your own agenda, and what it is that you want to say or tell them, just listen. When someone is hurting, they want to be heard, to know that there is another human being out there who hears them and acknowledges their existence. If you are thinking about what to say or do next, have you heard the client? Listen *and* hear before you act or respond.

The client knows you are listening if you take notes, and you can interject minimal responses—yes, okay, wow, really, I didn't know that, hmm, can you say that again?, interesting, super, that's wonderful, that's sad, and gee—to reinforce your attentive listening. Make eye contact, or look in the direction of the client since some clients become uncomfortable with eye contact. An expectant look and posture mean you are listening.

There are some who feel in a Rogerian sense, that "unconditional positive regard" is the single most effective thing that a therapist can do. Probably, so listen!

Minimalism

This is connected to listening since you can only use minimalist interjections and responses if you are paying exquisite attention to the client. You need to be able to read body language, and the smallest changes therein. The words to use as responses and for moving the client along are those listed in 'Listen' above. Masters of this approach, such as E. L. Rossi, are quite effective. The expectation is that clients left to their own devices and encouraged by the minimal responses and directions of the therapist will find their own unique solutions. This is both a kind of faith healing and psychological judo.

Crystal Ball

Erickson developed this approach to a fine art. It can be used within hypnosis and without. The client is asked to, "Please close your eyes, and go forward into the future to a time when all of the things that have been troubling you, and you came to see me about, have been resolved to your satisfaction. Looking back, what is it that I did, or you did, or we did, that brought about these changes?" The surprising thing is that they will tell you! Another way is, "Suppose you had a crystal ball that you could look into, and in which you could see yourself in the future after you have successfully overcome what it is that is bothering you, what do you see in there about how these changes came about?" (This is a form of the "miracle question".)

Metaphors

Ask the client to tell you a story about how they have changed. Then, re-tell them the story using their own words. You can use Metaphor Therapy or Guided Metaphor (see Chapter 13) or the traditional metaphoric method of telling stories that incorporate many possibilities for change. Remember, the more metaphoric and vague you are, the better—let the client fill in the details.

Ambiguous Function Assignments

When you are stuck, let an ambiguous function assignment be your helper. Have the client *do something* where you imply and expect they will find answers and solutions to what it is that had been concerning them. (Notice grammatical tenses.) The client does this strange thing and then discovers interesting answers unique to their circumstance (Chapter 11).

Look at Yourself From …

"I wonder what you will see and discover if you were to somehow be able to step outside of yourself, go behind me, look at yourself sitting there, and listen to what you have been telling me."

"What if, the next time you and your wife have an argument, you were able to step outside of yourself, and look and listen to yourself from the perspective of some place behind her. You are looking at yourself from over her shoulder. What would you notice about yourself and what you say and do and how you look?"

"The next time you are in that circumstance, step outside of yourself and observe yourself from another viewpoint. What do you notice?"

This is the Robert Burns approach of "seeing ourselves as others see us". This is not easy to do, but can certainly be enlightening.

Provocative Therapy

This approach was developed by Frank Farrelly and is described in the book by Farrelly and Brandsma (1974). This is one of my favorite "when all else fails" approaches. It involves being provocative in a humorous vein about the client's behaviors.

> "Are you really crazy, or are you just acting crazy?"
>
> "You are probably the fattest, sloppiest, saddest person I have ever met."
>
> "You are just plain stupid, you know. You don't know how to do anything right, you continually mess up, you don't use your brain (if you have one), and you are just a sorry excuse for an adult."

No one, but therapists, overlooks overt dysfunctional behavior in such forgiving ways. Farrelly calls a spade a spade and tells the client directly what the client already knows. Although this approach appears brutal on the surface, clients know that you are really paying attention to them because you are telling them the truth as they know it about themselves. This approach is not abusive, it is honest. There is an Erickson case where he tells a grossly obese client as she enters the door something like, "You are the fattest, grossest person I have ever seen." The client knew she could then trust Erickson! Provocative therapy is not for the faint-hearted therapist, and does need practice (and acting skills!).

Refer/Consult

When you are working with a client and do not know what to do, you can ask for consultations and supervision. Get someone more experienced and outside of the immediate situation to help you.

Working in a setting with colleagues available from behind a one-way mirror can be quite helpful. Regular supervision is helpful. And, if you feel you cannot help this client, it is only professional and ethical to refer them to another therapist.

If Erickson and the conversationalist in the first paragraph of this chapter admit that there are clients they cannot help or work with, then ...

When all else fails, do something different! Please.

Chapter 19
Brief Final Thoughts

This book has turned out to be shorter than I had anticipated—maybe I just got carried away with the very brief idea. There are a number of disciplines that presuppose the possibilities of single-session therapy and very brief therapy. This, of course, makes great economic sense to the client and third-party payers. If you have to make your living working this way, then you will spend quite a bit of time rustling up clients. Since I am retired and have a quite adequate pension, there is no economic incentive for me to prolong treatment. I get my satisfaction in working this way to find out just how fast I can help people. One of the presuppositions in this work is that permanent change can happen rapidly. If this is my belief, can the client be far behind? A dissatisfaction, since I do not feel it is professionally proper for me to follow up on clients and ask them how they are doing (this has overtones of soliciting them to come back for additional sessions), is that most of my very brief therapy clients just "disappear". They have been told at that last session that I would like to hear from them in a week or two to find out how they are doing. They rarely do this. On the other hand, I live in a small town (population of about 4000), and run into my clients in social and community events, and in the downtown stores. We smile or nod at each other and, that is that. Occasionally, to my satisfaction, at periods of one to several years at one of these happenstance meetings, a client will tell me how much they were helped back then! Aside from the probably unreliable lighter and happier state I perceive with which they leave that final session, I cannot offer the reader solid evidence that what I have written about in this book really works.

There are lots of ideas for interventions and things to do throughout the book. I have been selective in the sense that these are the things that I do, generally several of them in any given session. I like having lots of choices in what I do and how I do it. I really like the idea of working in an open-ended fashion with no time limits. And, I also like the simplicity of working on a cash basis so I do not have to write reports to third-parties or complicate my life and the life of the client by doing diagnoses. I occasionally tell clients that I have one diagnosis for everyone, and that is that they are temporarily troubled. That's enough, and it sets the stage for rapid change. If you have to do psychotherapy for a living, and if you have to deal with third parties, I hope that my philosophy is not too disturbing to you. And, remember, I do have a few clients I see for several sessions.

19.1 The Universal Very Brief Therapy Intervention (UVBTI[3])

I recently came across a six-step intervention for weight control. When something like this crosses my desk, I always question the *number* of steps—what if it were five or seven? I therefore thought it would be fitting in this final chapter to leave you with a one-step universal very brief therapy intervention—UVBTI. This intervention has its roots in Erickson's work, torpedo therapy, and other approaches. What is essential for its effectiveness is that the therapist needs to sincerely and congruently convey his/her conviction that this will work. The following intervention is designed for weight control—you can use your skills to adapt it to other behavioral changes, as well as to whatever concern(s) the client brings to the session. In my experience, permanent habit changes are similar to instantaneous religious conversions—an inner switch is flipped, and an irrevocable decision is made. Change can be and is that fast. The therapist facilitates this inner conversion process. Pauses are important, as well as the style of delivery.

The Universal Very Brief Therapy Intervention (UVBTI)

Well, Fred, there is a rapid way to help you with weight control. I know that you already know all that you need to know about how to do this, don't you? Good. You recall that we have talked earlier

---

[3] Every new intervention needs an acronym!

about the physiology of weight control. Good. So, sitting there comfortably, please close your eyes [or leave them softly unfocused], and take a few relaxing breaths. ... Somewhere out in front of you there is a black board or a white board. Something is written on that board, although you cannot read it as yet. Just to confirm, would you nod your head "yes" or say the word "yes" to let me know that at this time you are ready to control your weight for the rest of your life? [Assuming a "yes" signal] Thank you. Now, on that board—which you still cannot read—is a date: a day, a month and a year. That is the date by which you will have attained that new permanent weight, the one you will be able to maintain, for your health and wellbeing, for the rest of your life. Please read that date to yourself. This is your date, your time, your change ... and you can keep that date secret, storing it away in a secure place within your mind. No one else needs to know it. Your decision, your change, your knowledge. And, you do know, do you not, that you can and will do this? Again, just to confirm, nod "yes" or say the word "yes" to let me know that you know deep inside ... that you have already made the commitment, that internal decision, to do this by that date. [Assuming a "yes" signal] Thank you. Take a few moments now to consolidate what it is you have done for yourself. ... And, when you are ready, you can take a deep breath or two, stretch, and come back to this room.... Thank you.

Thanks for letting me share my style of working with you ...

References

American Psychiatric Association, 1994, *Diagnostic and statistical manual of mental disorders.* (4th edn). Washington, D.C.: American Psychiatric Association.

Andreas, S., and Andreas, C., 1987, *Change your mind and keep the change.* Moab, UT: Real People Press.

Bandler, R., and Grinder, J., 1975, *The structure of magic: I. A book about language and therapy.* Palo Alto, CA: Science and Behavior Books, Inc.

Bandler, R., and Grinder, J., 1982, *Reframing: Neuro-linguistic programming and the transformation of meaning.* Moab, UT: Real People Press.

Bateson, G., 1979, *Mind and nature: A necessary unity.* New York: E. P. Dutton.

Battino, R., 2000, *Guided imagery and other approaches to healing.* Carmarthen, UK: Crown House Publishing.

Battino, R., 2002, *Metaphoria: Metaphor and guided metaphor for psychotherapy and healing.* Carmarthen, UK: Crown House Publishing.

Battino, R., and South, T. L., 2005, *Ericksonian approaches: A comprehensive manual* (2nd edn). Carmarthen, UK: Crown House Publishing.

Berg, I. K., and Dolan, Y., 2001, *Tales of solutions: A collection of hope-inspiring stories.* New York: W. W. Norton & Co.

Beutler, L., and Clarkin, J., 1990, *Systematic treatment selection: Toward targeted therapeutic interventions.* New York: Brunner/Mazel.

Bodenhamer, B. G., and Hall, L. M., 1999, *The user's manual for the brain: The complete manual for neuro-linguistic programming practitioner certification*. Carmarthen, UK: Crown House Publishing.

Brown, J., Dreis, S., and Nace, D. K., 1999, "What really makes a difference in psychotherapy outcome? Why does managed care want to know?", in M. A. Hubble, B. L. Duncan, and S. D. Miller (eds), *The heart and soul of change: What works in psychotherapy* (pp. 389–406). Washington, D.C.: American Psychological Association.

Burns, G. W., 1998, *Nature-guided therapy: Brief integrative strategies for health and well-being*. New York: Brunner/Mazel (Taylor & Francis Group).

Cade, B., and O'Hanlon, W. H., 1993, *A brief guide to brief therapy*. New York: W. W. Norton & Co.

Cheek, D. B., 1994, *Hypnosis: The application of ideomotor techniques*. Needham Heights, MA: Allyn and Bacon.

Cheek, D. B., and LeCron, L. M., 1968, *Clinical hypnotherapy*. New York: Grune & Stratton.

Clement, P. W., 1994, "Quantitative evaluation of 26 years of private practice", *Professional Psychology: Research and Practice*, 25, 2, 173–6.

de Shazer, S., 1985, *Keys to solution in brief therapy*. New York: W. W. Norton & Co.

de Shazer, S., 1988, *Investigating solutions in brief therapy*. New York: W. W. Norton & Co.

de Shazer, S., 1994, *Words were originally magic*. New York: W. W. Norton & Co.

Derks, L., 2005, *Social panoramas: Changing the unconscious landscape with NLP and psychotherapy*. Carmarthen, UK: Crown House Publishing.

Duncan, B. L., and Miller, S. D., 2000, *The heroic client: Doing client-directed, outcome-informed therapy*. San Francisco: Jossey-Bass.

Duncan, B. L., Miller, S. D., and Sparks, J. A., 2004, *The heroic client: A revolutionary way to improve effectiveness through client-directed, outcome-informed therapy*. San Francisco: Jossey-Bass.

Epston, D., and White, M., 1992, *Experience, contradiction, narrative, & imagination: Selected papers of David Epston & Michael White. 1989–1991*. Adelaide: Dulwich Centre Publications.

Erickson, M. H., and Rossi, E. L., 1979, *Hypnotherapy: An exploratory casebook*. New York: Irvington Publishers, Inc.

Erickson, M. H., Rossi, E. L., and Rossi, S. I., 1976, *Hypnotic realities*. New York: Irvington Publishers, Inc.

Farrelly, F., and Brandsma, J., 1974, *Provocative therapy*. San Francisco: Shields Publishing Co.

Frank, J. D., 1995, "Psychotherapy as rhetoric: Some implications", *Clinical Psychology: Science and Practice*, 2, 90–3.

Frank, J. D., and Frank, J. B., 1991, *Persuasion and healing: A comparative study of psychotherapy* (3rd edn). Baltimore: Johns Hopkins University Press.

Freedman, J., and Combs, G., 1996, *Narrative therapy: The social construction of preferred realities*. New York: W. W. Norton & Co.

Friedman, H. J., 1963, "Patient expectancy and symptom reduction", *Archives of General Psychiatry*, 8, 61–7.

Garfield, S., 1986, "Problems in diagnostic classification." In T. Millon and G. Klerman (eds), *Contemporary directions in psychopathology*. New York: Guilford Press.

Gilligan, S. G., 1987, *Therapeutic trances: The cooperation principle in Ericksonian hypnotherapy*. New York: Brunner/Mazel.

Goldstein, A. P., 1960, "Patients' expectancies and non-specific therapy as a basis for (un)spontaneous remission", *Journal of Clinical Psychology, 16*, 399–403.

Greenberg, R. P., and Fisher, S., 1997, "Mood-mending medicines: Probing drug, psychotherapy, and placebo solutions", in S. Fisher and R. P. Greenberg (eds), *From placebo to panacea: Putting psychiatric drugs to the test* (pp. 115–72). New York: Wiley.

Grencavage, L. M., and Norcross, J. C., 1990, "Where are the commonalities among the therapeutic common factors?" *Professional Psychology: Research and Practice, 21*, 372–8.

Grinder, J., and Bandler, R., 1976, *The structure of magic II*. Palo Alto, CA: Science and Behavior Books, Inc.

Grinder, J., and Bandler, R., 1981, *Trance-formations: Neuro-linguistic programming and the structure of hypnosis*. Moab, UT: Real People Press.

Grissom, R. J., 1996, "The magical number 7 ± 2: Meta-meta-analysis of the probability of superior outcome in comparisons involving therapy, placebo, and control", *Journal of Consulting and Clinical Psychology, 64*, 973–82.

Haley, J., 1963, *Strategies of psychotherapy*. New York: Grune and Stratton.

Haley, J., 1984, *Ordeal therapy: Unusual ways to change behavior*. San Francisco: Jossey-Bass Publishers.

Hall, E. T., 1959, *The silent language*. New York: A Fawcett Premier Book (Doubleday & Co., Inc.).

Hall, L. M., and Bodenhamer, B. G., 2003, *The user's manual for the brain Volume II: Mastering systemic NLP*. Carmarthen, UK: Crown House Publishing.

Hammerschlag, C. A., and Silverman, H. D., 1997, *Healing ceremonies: Creating personal rituals for spiritual, emotional, physical and mental health*. New York: A Perigree Book.

Howard, K. I., Kopte, S. M., Krause, M. S., and Orlinsky, D. E., 1986, "The dose-effect relationship in psychotherapy", *American Psychologist*, 41(2), 159–64.

Hubble, M. A., Duncan, B. L., and Miller, S. D. (eds), 1999, *The heart & soul of change: What works in therapy*. Washington, DC: American Psychological Association.

James, T., and Woodsmall, W., 1988, *Time line therapy and the basis of personality*. Cupertino, CA: Meta Publications.

Jerstad, L., and Stelzer, J., 1973, "Adventure experiences as treatment for residential mental patients", *Therapeutic Recreation Journal*, 7(3), 8–11.

Kane, S., and Olness, K. (eds), 2004, *The art of therapeutic communication: The collected works of Kay F. Thompson*. Carmarthen, UK: Crown House Publishing.

Kopp, R. R., 1995, *Metaphor therapy: Using client-generated metaphors in psychotherapy*. New York: Brunner/Mazel.

Kutchins, K., and Kirk, H., 1997, *Making us crazy:* DSM: *The psychiatric bible and the creation of mental disorders*. New York: Free Press.

Lambert, M. J., 1992, "Psychotherapy outcome research: Implications for integrative and eclectic therapists", in J. C. Norcross and M. R. Goldfried (eds), *Handbook of psychotherapy integration*. (pp. 94–129). New York: Basic Books.

Lambert, M. J., and Ogles, B., 2004, "The efficacy and effectiveness of psychotherapy", in M. J. Lambert (ed), *Bergin and Garfield's handbook of psychotherapy and behavior change* (5th ed, pp. 139–93). New York: Wiley.

Lankton, S. R., and Lankton, C. H., 1986, *Enchantment and intervention in family therapy: Training in Ericksonian approaches*. New York: Brunner/Mazel.

LeCron, L. M., 1964, *Self hypnotism*. New York: New American Library.

Lowry, T. P., 1974, "Camping as a short term psychiatric hospital", in T. P. Lowry (ed), *Camping therapy: Its uses in psychiatry and rehabilitation*. Springfield, IL: Charles C. Thomas.

Miller, S. D., and Berg, I. K., 1995, *The miracle method: A radically new approach to problem drinking*. New York: W. W. Norton & Co.

Miller, S. D., and Duncan, B. L., 2000, *The Outcome Rating Scale* [Online]. Available: http://www.talkingcure.com/measures.htm.

Miller, S. D., Hubble, M. A., and Duncan, B. L., 1996, *Handbook of solution-focused brief therapy*. San Francisco: Jossey-Bass Publishers.

Monk, G. Winslade, J., Crocket, K., and Epston, D. (eds), 1997, *Narrative therapy in practice: The archeology of hope*. San Francisco: Jossey-Bass Publishers.

O'Hanlon, W. H., 1987, *Taproots: Underlying principles of Milton Erickson's therapy and hypnosis*. New York: W. W. Norton & Co.

O'Hanlon, W. H., 1994, "The third wave", *Family Therapy Networker*, Nov/Dec, 19–29.

O'Hanlon, B., 2003, *A guide to inclusive therapy: 26 methods of respectful resistance-dissolving therapy*. New York: W. W. Norton & Co.

O'Hanlon, B., and Beadle, S., 1997, *A guide to possibility land: Fifty-one methods for doing brief, respectful therapy*. New York: W. W. Norton & Co.

O'Hanlon, W. H., and Martin, M., 1992, *Solution-oriented hypnosis: An Ericksonian approach*. New York: W. W. Norton & Co.

O'Hanlon, B., and Rowan, T., 2003, *Solution oriented therapy for chronic and severe mental illness*. New York: W. W. Norton & Co.

O'Hanlon, B., and Wilk, J., 1987, *Shifting contexts: The generation of effective psychotherapy*. New York: The Guilford Press.

O'Hanlon, W. H., and Weiner-Davis, M., 1989, *In search of solutions: A new direction in psychotherapy*. New York: W. W. Norton & Co.

Pelletier, K. R., 1977, *Mind as healer, mind as slayer*. New York: Delacorte Press.

Pelletier, K. R., 1978, *Toward a science of consciousness*. New York: Delacorte Press.

Remen, R. N., 1996, *Kitchen table wisdom: Stories that heal*. New York: Riverhead Books.

Rosen, S., 1982, *My voice will go with you: The teaching tales of Milton H. Erickson, M.D.* New York: W. W. Norton & Co.

Rosenzweig, S., 1936, "Some implicit common factors in diverse methods of psychotherapy; 'At last,' the Dodo said, 'Everybody has won and all must have prizes' ", *American Journal of Orthopsychiatry*, 6, 412–15.

Rossi, E. L., 1993, *The psychobiology of mind-body healing: New concepts of therapeutic hypnosis* (2nd edn). New York: W. W. Norton & Co.

Rossi, E. L., 1996, *The symptom path to enlightenment: The new dynamics of self-organization in hypnotherapy: An advanced manual for beginners*. Pacific Palisades, CA: Palisades Gateway Publishing.

Rossi, E. L., 2002, *The psychobiology of gene expression: Neuroscience and neurogenesis in hypnosis and the healing arts*. New York: W. W. Norton & Co.

Rossi, E. L., 2005, *A discourse with our genes: The psychosocial and cultural genomics of therapeutic hypnosis and psychotherapy*. Phoenix: Zeig, Tucker & Theisen, Inc.

Rossi, E. L., and Cheek, D. B., 1988, *Mind–body therapy: Ideodynamic healing in hypnosis*. New York: W. W. Norton & Co.

Rossi, E. L., and Nimmons, D., 1991, *The 20-minute break*. Los Angeles: Jeremy P. Tarcher, Inc.

Salovey, P., and Turk, D., 1991, "Clinical judgment and decision making", in C.R. Snyder and D.R. Forsyth (eds), *Handbook of social and clinical psychology: The health perspective* (pp. 416–37). New York: Pergamon.

Short, D., Erickson, B. A., and Erickson Klein, R., 2005, *Hope & resiliency: Understanding the psychotherapeutic strategies of Milton H. Erickson, MD*. Carmarthen, UK: Crown House Publishing Limited.

Snyder, E. D., 1971, *Hypnotic poetry: A study of trance-inducing technique in certain poems and its literary significance*. New York: Octagon Books.

Talmon, M., 1990, *Single-session therapy: Maximizing the effect of the first (and often only) therapeutic encounter*. San Francisco: Jossey-Bass.

Ulrich, R. S., 1984, "View through a window may influence recovery from surgery", *Science, 224*, 420–1.

Ulrich, R. S., Dimberg, U., and Driver, B., 1991, "Psychophysiological indicators", in B. Driver, P. Brown, and G. Peterson (eds), *Benefits of leisure*. State College, PA: Venture.

Wampold, B. E., 2001, *The great psychotherapy debate: Models, methods, and findings*. Mahwah, NJ: Lawrence Erlbaum Associates, Publishers.

Watzlawick, P., Weakland, J., and Fisch, R., 1974, *Change: Principles of problem formation and problem resolution*. New York: W. W. Norton & Co.

Weiner-Davis, M., de Shazer, S., and Gingerich, W. J., 1987, "Building pretreatment change to construct the therapeutic solution: An exploratory study", *Journal of Marital and Family Therapy, 13*, 359–63.

White, M., 1995, *Re-authoring lives: Interviews and essays*. Adelaide: Dulwich Centre Publications.

White, M., and Epston, D., 1990, *Narrative means to therapeutic ends.* New York: W. W. Norton & Co.

Woodsmall, W., 1989, *Lifeline therapy.* Arlington, VA: Advance Behavior Modeling.

Zeig, J. K. (ed), 1980, *Teaching seminar with Milton H. Erickson, M.D.* New York: Brunner/Mazel.

Index